Humans in the
Natural World

THIRD EDITION

Shoshanah Jacobs
Jillian Bergstrome
Eric Harvey
Lauren Overdyk

Kendall Hunt
publishing company

Cover image © Shutterstock.com

Kendall Hunt
publishing company

www.kendallhunt.com
Send all inquiries to:
4050 Westmark Drive
Dubuque, IA 52004-1840

Published in the United States of America

Dedication

This book is dedicated to the students of BIOL*1500
at the University of Guelph: you asked for it!

Contents

I have been privileged to have had some wonderful teaching assistants along the journey of teaching Humans in the Natural World. They have come from such different backgrounds and each one has contributed in some important way to the development of the course. In the Fall of 2013, Lauren, Jill, and Eric were the teaching assistants assigned to this course. Lauren had been with this course since it began in its current form, Eric was assigned for the first time, and Jill was a late addition as the course became so popular that enrollment increased by about 40%! What a team! We decided to write this book together. You will see, by their biographies, that they have such different backgrounds and different voices. I hope that their voices have been preserved in these pages and that you enjoy reading them.

SJ

Eric Harvey

I do what I do because of a passionate thirst to understand the world that surrounds me. I have vast interests in anthropology, history, physics,

and philosophy, but I choose ecology because of its unequalled complexity. What can be more generalizable, more challenging, more satisfying than understanding how interactions among different entities are shaped and how this network of interactions can, in turn, shape the dynamics and functioning of natural systems?

Most of all I think that doing science is not about being good in math, rather it is about passion and creativity, it is about reading the past, understanding the present, and dreaming up a tomorrow. I wrote this chapter hoping to illustrate that ideas, like species, are not spontaneously created. They have deep roots in the past, they evolve, they adapt, they merge, they go extinct, and most of all they are what binds the past with the future.

Passion for science is not always something clearly defined, especially when as a child you have no interest in mathematics or physics. I always had an interest for understanding the world around me; however, being raised in a Catholic family, this passion was mainly expressed through spirituality. No discipline had more impacts on who I am than history and philosophy. History brings perspective and philosophy gives the tool to rationally resonate this perspective into new ideas. In parallel, I grew up with an admiration for "Nature," its beauty, its working, and its complexity. "Nature" as a conceptual challenge, and also as a playground. Still, I thought that science was not for me, and it is not until the very last moment, one month before starting my politics and anthropology degree that I decided to take biology instead. To this day I have never regretted that choice. The passions for physics, statistics, and all other scientific disciplines followed naturally, as essential tools to understand the world better.

Sadly they do not teach science this way at school. The truth is that science should always be singular as there is only one science. The sub-scientific disciplines are nothing more than necessary reductionism. All types of knowledge are fulfilling and I cannot encourage more anyone who pursues knowledge to do so passionately. Passion is not an intangible concept; it is the very root of our capacity to transform the world around us.

Lauren Overdyk

My name is Lauren and I am from Toronto, Ontario. I grew up in the suburbs, but was lucky enough to spend a lot of time up north in Gravenhurst, Ontario, exploring Riley Lake. Here I learned about frogs and fish and got to get my hands dirty with things most children do not get a chance to experience.

From a young age, I have always been intrigued by marine biology and, after watching the movie "Free Willy," I decided that the marine environment is where I belonged. I packed up and did my undergraduate degree in marine biology at the University of British Columbia, Vancouver, British Columbia. Here I got to experience sea life at its finest. I volunteered at the Vancouver Aquarium and had a chance to work at a marine

mammal rescue centre rehabilitating injured and abandoned harbour seals. During my summers off, I worked in the conservation world in Ontario collecting baseline information on fish distribution and abundance in several of Ontario's watersheds. It is here that I rediscovered my love for freshwater fish. I later travelled to New Zealand where I completed a postgraduate diploma studying a fissiparous sea star *Allostichaster polyplax*.

Following this, I decided to re-enter the academic life and came to work at the University of Guelph doing my PhD on the ecologically and commercially important fish species Lake White-fish (*Coregonus clupeaformis*). I am nearly done my PhD and am not sure where the next chapter of my life will take me. I would love to continue my work with freshwater fish and answering key ecological questions about Great Lakes species.

My advice to you, if you are an aspiring scientist or graduate student, is the following:

1) Do your homework! Make sure you thoroughly research the university, the professor, and the program you are about to undertake. Doing a PhD is an incredible commitment, mentally, financially, emotionally, and in time.
2) Stay passionate about what you are doing! There will be ups and downs, but if you love what you are studying and love what you are doing then it will all work out in the end.
3) Be yourself! You will encounter a lot of different characters along your journey— some will help you, some will be obstacles to overcome. As long as you know you have done your best and have been true to yourself, you can survive it all.

Jillian Bergstrome

Like many children, I spent a large amount of my childhood getting lost in the woods and exploring the world. I developed a love and interest for all things in nature from forests, and travelling instilled a fascination with the world as well as gave

me ambition to keep adventuring. Growing up on the St. Lawrence River, I always felt at home in the water. By the age of 13, I had experience scuba diving in the ocean and rehabilitating Pygmy Sperm whales, which led to me to the University of Guelph Marine and Freshwater Biology program.

Partway through my schooling I took advantage of the opportunity to study abroad, combining my love for learning and travel. While at the University of Konstanz in Germany, I focused on Human Physiology and Toxicology. I then dabbled in Marine Engineering in the following semester at Griffith University in Australia.

Following my excursions abroad, I returned to the University of Guelph and switched to General Sciences program. In the last two years of my undergraduate career I spent my summers collecting insects in National Parks across Canada for the Barcode of Life project. During the school semester, I was employed at the connected Biodiversity Institute of Ontario sampling insects and helping with mathematical calculations. In the final year of my undergraduate I completed a Bachelors thesis in Physiology with Dr. Bernier, investigating the effects of oxygen levels on the production of stress peptides in the hearts of zebrafish.

After completing my undergraduate program, I launched straight into my Master's degree under the combined supervision of Dr. Bernier and Dr. Van Der Kraak. During this time, I learned the joys of teaching through being one of Dr. Jacobs' teaching assistants for the Humans in the Natural World course. Shortly after assisting with Dr. Jacob's course, I decided to take a leave from the long road of academia to pursue my passion of the outdoors. Currently, I work as a manager and instructor at a climbing gym in Guelph and in my spare time I take adventurous nature enthusiasts caving, ice climbing, and rock climbing.

I feel honored to have been worked with Dr. Jacobs, Eric, and Lauren, as well as extremely grateful to have been involved in teaching the Humans in the Natural World course. Being able to work with passionate young people that are eager to learn and have such a passion for life has been one of the most fulfilling experiences of my life. My advice to you is keep doing what you are doing! Find what excites you and what you are passionate about and immerse yourself in it.

Introduction

September, 2012 was the first offering of "Humans in the Natural World" with this curriculum. When I designed the course, my goal was to teach science to non-science majors in a way that did not feel like I was reinforcing the stereotypes that unfortunately still follow us around. My goal was to demonstrate that we are all familiar with the scientific method and that our tendency towards biophilia (attraction to biological things) could be harnessed to develop an appreciation for biological systems and, maybe, even science.

The course and this book are divided into some seemingly random chapters. We start first by exploring how to think like a scientist. Then we think about the concept of niche and ecosystems. Then we dive into cells, genetics, and evolution. You may feel like there is no connection. When this happens, we will be halfway through the course! But bear with us. You see, we need to learn to think like a scientist so that we can appreciate all that is to come in the course. Everything that we tell you about was discovered using the scientific method. We need to be able to appreciate the information not only for its "truth" but also for its weaknesses. We want to supply you with the tools to be critical in a way that is constructive.

Learning about niche concept is a challenge. In fact, it is the only really confusing thing that students have struggled with, so we urge you to ensure that you are not making cross-disciplinary assumptions. A niche defines our place in the ecosystem. It is what we represent to other organisms and to the non-living components of the natural world. Every living thing has a niche and we understand niche to understand how everything is connected. Learning about niche gives us a starting point for talking about the human place in the natural world and how it has fundamentally changed.

Then evolution. To quote the definitive cliché of biology "Nothing in biology makes sense except in the light of evolution." Theodosius Dobzhansky could not have said it better. We are going to explore evolution from the DNA all the way up to the species, and maybe even further! We are going to figure out how change happens, why, and when. And we will speculate on what might happen in the future.

And then we are ready to begin. We will start at the very beginning with the first molecule that could reproduce itself and we will explore the complexity that can arise from repeated building blocks called cells. We will learn about important biological paradigm shifts that allowed for even more variety and we will tiptoe around trying to answer the "why?"

When we get to "human," we will slow down. We will learn about how we were when we first arrived on the evolutionary scene. We will explore which tools we had and which ones we invented, and we will consider the impact of our biology on the planet. We will take some random paths off the main road to talk about language, culture, and religion. But we will always try to understand it using the scientific tools and concepts that we armed ourselves with at the beginning.

This text is not finished. We began writing it after we had heard "we need a textbook" many many times for our students. In the Fall 2013 semester, we asked students for more details. They told us to make it fun, make it interesting, make it accessible, and make it affordable.

Reading this book alone will not ensure that you pass the course. Answering the questions and working through the problems will most certainly help. But you may not find the "answers" in the text. You may have to practise your searching skills to find the answer. And there may not be a single right answer. This does not mean that you can easily skip that question and move on because it is not likely to appear on an exam. On the contrary, the process of trying to answer a multifaceted question will hopefully teach you all sorts of things that can be examined later on! We will be using class time to reinforce and explore further. This text is just the beginning of a conversation that we have the distinct pleasure of having with you.

Shoshanah Jacobs
Jillian Bergstrome
Eric Harvey
Lauren Overdyk

p.s. The proceeds from the sales of this text are used to offer undergraduate students the opportunity to conduct independent research on questions that are of interest to them.

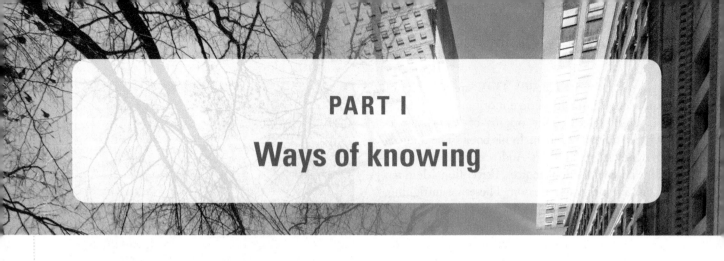

PART I
Ways of knowing

How do we *know* what we know? Is one way *better* than another? What are the consequences of using one form of acquiring knowledge over another? Do we, for example, end up with the same result if we use different methods? There are no definitive answers to any of these questions but there is a continuously growing body of literature that addresses the creation, management, manipulation, and dissemination of knowledge often referred to as KTT (knowledge translation and transfer). In light of the recent political, social, and economic events, an individual understanding of the source of knowledge and an ability to critically evaluate its reliability has become essential. In fact, over the last decade, we have witnessed the increasing importance in teaching KTT to undergraduate students. It has become the new vital "skill set" as traditional content-based education becomes obsolete with the growing availability of free information. Universities were once where students acquired information but now the internet largely serves this function. What we can still offer in an undergraduate education is training in processing, managing, critiquing, and acting upon this information. This is KTT.

But are there "types" of knowledge? Can they be broken down into categories and managed in meaningful ways to distinguish among them? The answer is 'yes' but nobody agrees on how to do it. Some philosophers start with Personal Knowledge, Procedural (a.k.a Ability) Knowledge, and Propositional Knowledge.

Personal Knowledge is that which pertains one's self, including personal taste and preference. "Blue is my favourite colour" is an example, as is "It really bothers me when you put itching powder in my bed."

Procedural Knowledge describes protocols and recipes, knowledge that pertains to getting something done. This is an interesting category because it does not include knowing the theory behind something, but, rather, knowing how to actually do it. Therefore, it requires memory of the "recipe" but also muscle memory of the action.

Propositional Knowledge refers to the knowledge of fact.

It is the third "type" that is relevant to our exploration of knowledge. To me, the other two types (Personal and Procedural) can be argued to also be Propositional. Having a background in science, it is difficult for me to view these categories as being distinct and of equal value. Part of me wants to say "well, who cares what my favourite colour is?" and to ask, instead, "how do I know what my favourite colour is?" To me, it is the second question that is more interesting. To answer this question though, we need to collect facts, facts about my response to different colours. This is propositional knowledge.

But what if, instead of collecting facts about how different colours make me react, I was simply informed that my favourite colour is turquoise, or, similarly, a bunch of people get together and, after watching me for several days, perhaps monitoring my choice of clothing, or the colours that I chose in the pictures I was drawing, simply declared that my favourite colour must be lime green (indeed, it is my favourite colour!). These are also bits of knowledge, but with different origins.

Understanding the origins of knowledge is what distinguishes them. In his book "The Sources of Knowledge," Robert Audi categorizes knowledge based upon four sources: Perception, Memory, Consciousness, and Reason. These are intriguing. Perception Knowledge is that which can be gathered by using one's senses, in the moment. It is different from Memory Knowledge because it can be generated immediately, without prior knowledge. Memory Knowledge is "stored." But in order for it to be "stored," it had to come from somewhere other than memory. Perception, perhaps. And this is an example of the inherent difficulty in classifying knowledge. But this system is intriguing because it suggests that one's experience and context are relevant information (Memory and Consciousness) and should be considered.

From a historical perspective, classifying knowledge becomes quite elementary. Indeed, it is also biologically relevant because knowledge, its origin, and its use have contributed to the success of our species and have, in turn, moulded our anatomy. From a temporal perspective, therefore, we can identify three key categories of (propositional) knowledge. These are **Traditional**, **Faith**, and **Science** Knowledge.

Traditional Knowledge

The term Traditional Knowledge can be used in several ways and it is important to distinguish among them. Some people restrict it to the body of knowledge that originates from Indigenous or "traditional" societies. Others define it more by how it is generated rather than who generates it. There are important consequences to this distinction especially in the context of the rapid loss of Indigenous cultures around the world. If we limit our definition of Traditional Knowledge to these cultures, and if the futures of these cultures are threatened, does this mean that Traditional Knowledge is also threatened? If you were to search the scholarly literature with the keywords "Traditional Knowledge," what pops up are article related to the

A craftsman repairs a saddle. The shape and functionality of the saddle were not developed by the scientific method, but rather over time, by observation and consensus among many people. It is an example of the "product" of Traditional Knowledge.

use of Indigenous traditional knowledge in environmental policy. Go ahead, try it.

The Assembly of First Nations defines Traditional Knowledge as "*The collective knowledge of traditions used by Indigenous groups to sustain and adapt themselves to their environment over time.*" Note here that this definition does restrict Traditional Knowledge to Indigenous groups. What is more intriguing about this definition is that it incorporates a *use* of that knowledge that is very biological. The word "adapt" suggests that knowledge is used for change and survival, to respond to a changing environment, to evolve. And, indeed, this is the *function* of knowledge generally. For humans, knowledge is used as a means of surviving in a changing environment. It is what we use to be biologically successful, to find shelter, a mate, and produce offspring. So I'm not sure that the function of 'adapting to the environment' can be ascribed only to traditional knowledge. Perhaps one could argue that those who use traditional knowledge adapt more successfully, but that is another issue. But the larger issue here is that Traditional Knowledge is not only generated and managed by traditional cultures. I would like to challenge you to think on a bigger scale, to ask yourself, if Indigenous culture is synonymous with Traditional Knowledge, does this mean that non-Indigenous cultures do not use it? Or does it mean that they *also* use it?

Examples of really old Traditional Knowledge documentation are hard to come by. Some of the oldest cave paintings date back to only 38,000 years ago.

The World Intellectual Property Organization recognizes that traditional knowledge is not only generated by Indigenous cultures, but by all humans from all cultures with their definition "Knowledge, know-how, skills, and practises that are developed, sustained, and passed on from generation to generation within a community, often forming part of its cultural or spiritual identity." Here we see no reference to function, but we do see reference to *mechanism*. The word "developed" suggests that the creation of the "bits" of knowledge happens over time, combined with "passing on from generation to generation," that it happens with contributions from several individuals. Traditional knowledge is **built by consensus following observation**. It is the accumulation of facts from the environment and the moulding and merging of those facts into useful information in order to assist in survival whether proximate (i.e. this berry is poisonous) or ultimate (i.e. close community relationships will buffer us from environmental disturbance). It is not that only "traditional peoples" possess and deal in Traditional Knowledge but rather that most of us go about our lives managing these bits of traditional knowledge! It is not Science that tells us that walking out in the middle of a busy street without looking for traffic

> **Think about it . . .**
>
> Is the generation and use of Traditional Knowledge limited to Indigenous people? How so?
>
> _____
> _____
> _____
> _____
> _____
> _____

is likely to cause injury. This information was created by observation and consensus; it is Traditional Knowledge. No one needed to conduct a scientific experiment in order to conclude that traffic-walking is a dangerous activity just like the Indigenous New Guinean populations refuse to camp near dead trees despite the obvious shelter that they provide. You see, dead trees tend to fall and, as it turns out, death by dead tree is by far the most common way of dying in traditional New Guinea society. Traffic walking is not excluded from the body of Traditional Knowledge because it is not used by "traditional people"; it shares the same classification as dead tree camping because it originates from observation and consensus.

An important distinguishing characteristic that is relevant to the story of human evolution is that Traditional Knowledge is old. In fact, it is the oldest type of knowledge that we will be considering according to the categories presented. It is at least as old as the species *Homo sapiens sapiens* (so at least 195,000 years), but it is likely even older as further evidence becomes available supporting the notion that other Hominids also had sophisticated language and culture. And this is where it becomes further confused. Do we need language to have knowledge? If we strip the definitions of these two terms (language and knowledge) down to their very bare bones, then I suspect that the answer is no. With reference specifically to

European Grey Wolves hunt together using a complex system of non-verbal communication.

Chimpanzees have been known to use plants with medicinal properties to treat ailments. Indigenous populations have carefully observed their behaviour and have used these same plants to treat similar conditions.

Traditional Knowledge, the requirements do not necessitate language. Information can be created by consensus among individuals without language per se. There are many examples of organisms communicating among themselves without the use of language, of passing on that "knowledge" to other generations, and of modifying and improving it over time. So, one could argue that Traditional Knowledge is as old as the oldest form of communication.

But let us not get ahead of ourselves and simply say that language is required. When did language (as we know it to be) evolve? We know that humans, *Homo sapiens sapiens,* have had language (or, at least, the anatomy required to generate, develop, and use language) since they first appeared on the scene and so we can reasonably suspect that language evolved before humans. As we will see later, there is a growing body of evidence that Neanderthals (*Homo sapiens neanderthalis*) possessed complex language systems, further suggesting that they had rich Traditional Knowledge systems. If this is the case, then Traditional Knowledge in its complex form has been around for many hundreds of thousands of years before humans.

Mentioned previously was that the term Traditional Knowledge is now more commonly limited to the knowledge systems created and developed by Indigenous populations. We study these systems for many reasons and benefits to humanity, including to better understand the evolution of the larger-scale Traditional Knowledge as described above. The value of Indigenous knowledge systems cannot be overstated; medicinal treatments of ailments have been developed by traditional knowledge, and the fields of midwifery, ethnobotany, and celestial navigation are all derived from Traditional Knowledge bases.

Though now a "certified profession" based upon scientific evidence and practise, midwifery likely began in prehistoric times. Throughout history (up until recently, that is), women have assumed the powerful role of healer, including midwife and in most cultures this role was well respected. There is a paucity, generally, of archaeological evidence that extends into pre-history and perhaps the earliest evidence of a woman's role in healing and childbirth comes from the Sumerian civilization (2900–2350 BCE); a stone statue of a priestess holding a torch (the symbol of the midwife) was unearthed in the Tigris and Euphrates Valley.

Many plants possess medicinal properties that are known not only to humans, but also to other animals. In fact, it is likely that human use of plants and other things for medicinal purposes arose from the careful observation of other animals self-medicating. The most famous of examples comes from Gombe region of Nigeria where the populations of chimpanzees have been studied by animal behaviourists for decades since 1965. In an article published in 1983 by R.W. Wrangham and T. Nishida, there were field observations of chimpanzees consuming the leaves of the plant *Aspilia* spp. (common name: takan, Ivory Coast), a coarse perennial herb with a pale yellow flower found in the savannah grasslands or woodland areas of west tropical Africa. Moreover, they noticed that not only did these chimpanzees consume these leaves in a manner different than other leaves (they folded them and rolled them around in their mouths without chewing before swallowing them whole), but they often appeared as though this was not a pleasurable activity. Further research revealed that the leaves of *Aspilia* spp. are not a significant source of nutrition and that they are passed through the digestive system without signs of having been digested. Therefore, the chimpanzees were likely not consuming them as food. Further fecal analysis showed that often the tiny hairs of the leaves were covered in small intestinal worms, parasites to chimpanzees that cause discomfort.

Was this "Traditional Knowledge" of a natural medicine being passed on to humans and not just other chimpanzees? Indeed! When the researchers visited the local Indigenous populations, they discovered that *Aspilia* spp. was commonly used to treat a number of ailments including burns, wounds, and intestinal worms.

"Well, it's not surprising that chimpanzees show these occasional signs of possessing the ability to manage Traditional Knowledge given they are so genetically similar to humans!," you

may argue. And indeed, it is not that surprising (though it is pretty darn cool). But examples of animals using plants and other resources to treat ailments or to prevent them have been documented in less similar groups such as bears, cats, dogs, and elephants.

It seems that nowadays we do not invest much time in learning about traditional medicines from other animals, but the study of traditional medicine use by Indigenous populations is of vital importance to the future of medicine as a whole. Approximately 25% of all new drugs are derived from plants, representing billions of dollars in annual revenue in North America. A study in the 1980s on Chinese Traditional Medicine revealed that over 2,000 plant species are known to be used and in northern Thailand, over 500 species have known medicinal properties. Studying how people use plants as medicine derived from Traditional Knowledge systems is far more cost effective than screening all known species of plants. Which plants would we pick first? Upon which ailments would we study their effects? Traditional Knowledge is used as a "guide" by medical researchers to not only cut down on the cost associated with medical discovery, but also to decrease the time that it takes to develop effective treatments that could save lives.

As we further recognize the value of Traditional Knowledge for economic benefit, some difficult and interesting questions arise, including

A US patent granted for the use of turmeric for its wound-healing abilities sparked the creation of the Traditional Knowledge Digital Library in India to protect the culture's wealth of knowledge.

that of "ownership" of the information. The need for protecting this information or for keeping it within the public domain has been recognized and some remarkable solutions have been developed. The Traditional Knowledge Digital Library (TKDL) of India contains 2,260,000 medical formulas available to readers of several languages including English, French, German, Japanese, and Spanish. The necessity for this database was recognized when a US patent was awarded based on the wound-healing capabilities of turmeric (a plant native to southeast India used as a spice and for dyeing fabrics due to its bright orange colour). Even though the properties of turmeric have been known for a very long time, the patent was granted by the United States Patent and Trademark Office because the search conducted by the patent review office were not done in the languages associated with the descriptions of the turmeric technology, namely, Sanskrit, Hindi, Arabic, Urdu, and Tamil. Therefore, the search 'revealed' that the use of turmeric for the purposes of wound healing was indeed 'novel and not previously known.' In English.

The Council of Scientific and Industrial Research and the Department of Ayurveda, Yoga, and Naturopathy came together to fight this patent and have it revoked. At that time that the TKDL was created, it was estimated that 2,000 patents were filed annually for innovations derived from Traditional Indian Knowledge. This database, available to patent examiners around the world for a nominal fee, has now put a stop to this practise and has protected the knowledge base while making it readily available, open source.

So where is Traditional Knowledge headed? There seems to be a false dichotomy developing between Traditional Knowledge and Modern Knowledge. A quick search of internet content on "modern traditional knowledge," for example, reveals many links to pages discussing the importance of Traditional Knowledge in medicine, culture, and society, but it does not lead to pages that view Traditional Knowledge creation as an ongoing phenomenon. I think that this represents the larger view that Traditional Knowledge creation is dead. But how can it possibly be dead? If we go back to the stated conditions under which

Traditional Knowledge is developed, we see that the recipe requires 1) observation of the world around us and 2) consensus and 3) time. These things are not absent from our modern world and so Traditional Knowledge is alive and well.

Faith Knowledge

Faith Knowledge can also be confused with other concepts. With Traditional Knowledge we had to distinguish between the broader concept and that of Indigenous Knowledge, a subset of the category. With Faith Knowledge, we need to recognize the subset called Religious Knowledge and understand that religion is not a prerequisite of Faith Knowledge.

You can imagine that much has been written and debated on the subject of Faith Knowledge, especially with reference to religion. In 2003, Michael Hand wrote: "we count a person's beliefs as a matter of faith when they go beyond the evidence available, or are based on a reading of the evidence with which others may reasonably disagree." But Harvey Siegel (2003) says that the Hand (2003) definition is not enough because the belief must be held independent of the evidence and guarded against any evidence to the contrary: belief is "above" challenge. So you could conclude that Faith Knowledge requires protection. This protection is offered by an authority figure. In some cases, this authority could be a deity (and therefore falling into the subset of religious knowledge) while in many cases, this authority figure could be a community leader, such as a politician, or a prominent member of society such as a university professor. Furthermore, even a scientist can propagate Faith Knowledge. Here's why: Faith Knowledge is defined here as knowledge that is created, **over a short period of time, by an authority**. It is generally used to "explain" something or interpret significance. It is therefore quite possible that all of us, in some capacity, perhaps as a mother, or father, have passed on Faith Knowledge to others. Why is it that children believe in tooth fairies and bunnies with the ability to lay chocolate eggs? It is not because god or even a priest tells them, it is usually because a parent, a person of authority in that child's life, has told them of such things. And these characters, the tooth fairy, for example, was not "discovered" by observation, but were invented, over a short period of time by someone. It is not surprising that, when a child grows up and learns to question authority, these characters are often no longer believed to be real. But there are other positions of authority that are respected throughout a person's lifetime. Royalty, politicians, and leaders of industry are all considered authoritative and therefore have the ability to create and disseminate Faith Knowledge.

Dr. J. Sherman, an evolutionary epistomologist from Berkley and self-proclaimed non-authority, defines faith knowledge as "belief that is not based on proof." We could take this further and say that not only is it not based upon proof, in many cases, certainly in the case of religious knowledge, it *cannot* be confirmed with proof. If this is true, then Dr. Sherman's definition can be further simplified. Faith = belief. But we are not only talking about belief here. We are talking about knowledge that is created by an authority without a prescribed method, that is adopted by the user without consensus and without the ability to modify it. It is therefore the case that the use of Faith Knowledge is crucial to our survival as a species. Think of a newborn baby and what it requires to survive and grow. It is completely reliant upon its parent for food, shelter, warmth, and protection. Even as the

child grows and is able to speak, it relies upon the information that it receives from a parent. It does not add to it, generate it, or evaluate it. Without our ability to accept and use Faith Knowledge, our chances of survival beyond childhood would be greatly diminished. Parents become authorities (we often hear "because I said so" spoken to children!) and oftentimes the information increases the probability of survival of that child.

Because Faith Knowledge is created by an authority, some refer to it simply as Knowledge based upon Authority. It follows from this that the reputation of the authority as such is critical to their ability to create and disseminate that knowledge. If the authority is not or is no longer living, their reputation is likely to remain unaltered as is the case with a deity or martyr. If, however, that authority is a politician, business leader, or even a parent, he/she must continuously monitor their reputation to ensure their ability to remain recognized as an authority.

Science Knowledge

Science Knowledge is quite simply **knowledge that is generated by using the scientific method**. But, as we shall see, there are several permutations of the definition of the scientific method that can make the study of science philosophy delightful. Let us start at the beginning.

Both of these buildings represent the source of Faith Knowledge; whether it be knowledge from a politician (the Parliament Buildings on the left) or from a Priest (the Vatican on the right).

Though the scientific method as we know it today is likely only about 400 years old, the earliest reference to a standardized method of inquiry (answering a question) is the Edwin Smith Papyrus, dated at approximately 1700 BCE. Its value was first made known by American Edwin Smith, an Egypt-enthusiast of questionable reputation who acquired the manuscript by, perhaps, questionable means in 1862. Though Smith was the first to attempt translation, the document was not fully translated into English until 1930 when it became clear that this was indeed the oldest known "scientific" document and supported other evidence of Ancient Egypt having been a centre for advanced medicine of the time. Of the 48 medical cases presented in the manuscript, only 1 of them describes the use of a magical treatment. And, more notable than this, they are all presented with the following headings: Examination, Diagnosis, Treatment. This represents a repeatable, empirically inductive process that leads to a treatment and, hopefully, cure. What is perhaps even more exciting about this is that further analysis of the text suggests that it is a copy of another document originally written perhaps between 3000 and 2500 BCE.

But this case does not really allow us to distinguish this knowledge from Traditional Knowledge, because Traditional Knowledge is also created by empirical means (by direct or indirect observation). What is reminiscent of an component of the scientific method is that the cases are described in a consistent stepwise way suggesting the use of a repeated methodology.

Though only rarely acknowledged for his great contributions to science, the physicist al-Hassan Ibn al-Haitham could arguably be considered the Father of Modern Science. (This distinction usually goes to Thales of Miletus, a Greek philosopher who eschewed mysticism in the pursuit of knowledge.) Born in 965 AD in what is now Iraq, al-Hassan Ibn al-Haitham lived and worked during the time considered to be the Dark Ages in Europe, where not much seemed to have happened due to the collapse of the Western Roman Empire. Yet outside of Europe, and in particular within Arab society, intellectual advancement and technological civilization flourished. Using a combination of theoretical and experimental investigation, Al-Hassan Ibn al-Haitham proved that our eyes did not work by emitting light onto objects but rather by collecting light reflected off of surfaces around us. He studied the refraction of light by using lenses and mirrors and devised an explanation for the inner workings of the eye. This and many more discoveries were accomplished by using methodical experimentation and manipulation in order to logically eliminate the possible explanations for an observation until there was only one remaining. Truly a man of vast interests, it is thought that Al-Haitham wrote 200 publications (only 55 of which remain today) describing scientific discoveries that would pave the way for many great minds.

Thales of Miletus (640–546 BCE) has already been mentioned as a possible contender for the position of Father of Science because he was arguably one of the first pre-Socratic philosophers to suggest non-mythical explanations for natural observations. For example, Thales postulated that earthquakes were caused by the agitation of the water upon which the continents floated and not the ill-will of the god Poseidon. Yet, from what we know of Thales and his work, it was largely theoretical. Thales practised in the art of logic and so it follows that he would explore the non-mythical explanations. But, unlike Al-Haitham, there is no evidence of him having engaged in experimentation.

Perhaps a much more worthy rival for the title Father of Science is Aristotle (384–322 BCE). Aristotle made significant and lasting contributions in virtually all disciplines of science at the time and created a new one: zoology. It would be a book or two in itself to go through all of his work but the most relevant to our search for the Father of Science, is that Aristotle insisted that knowledge needed to be constructed upon a foundation of demonstration. Only 31 of his approximately 200 documents remain and these only in the form of notes. Through careful observation of biological models, such as the chicken, Aristotle developed the epigenetic theory, which countered the pre-formation theory. Pre-formation operates on the assumption that all the organ systems of a fertilized egg cell develop immediately and then incubation simply represents a period of growth. But Aristotle designed a carefully executed study whereby he cracked open fertilized chicken eggs at different stages of development and noticed that it was the heart that formed first, followed by the liver, etc. (had he a microscope, he would have actually seen the spine first). It followed from these observations that organs developed in a necessary hierarchy based on their function and the need for those functions to further development.

Approximately one-third of Aristotle's work was on the topic of Biology, a field that had been little explored until then. So perhaps, it is best to dub him the Father of Biology. But his contributions to the method of scientific inquiry, though they do not match the rigour of Al-Haitham's work, are indeed valuable.

Have you been wondering about the Mothers of Science? Or maybe you are wondering why I have chosen to use the word Father rather than Person. In a Wikipedia entry titled "List of people considered father or mother of a scientific field" (visited Oct. 2014), of the 192 people listed as "parents" in association with fields of science from acoustics to virology, 4 are women and all of them are considered to have made their contributions in "modern" times. Florence Nightingale (1820–1910) is the "earliest" on the list with her contributions to the field of nursing. She is known for having founded the profession of nursing through her innovative use of graphical statistics and her scientific approach to epidemiological questions. Literally writing the handbook on the field, *Notes on Nursing* (1859) was widely used as a textbook within the nursing schools of the time. Ellen Swallow Richards (1842–1911), the first female graduate of the Massachusetts Institute of Technology, is considered the Mother of Home Economics. A very successful industrial chemist, her work in sanitary engineering not only led to the creation of a new field of science, but also served as inspiration to other women to pursue an education in the sciences. The first woman to win a Nobel Prize and the first person to win two

Florence Nightingale (1820–1910) founded the professional field of nursing. This statue in London pays tribute to her contributions.

prizes, Marie Sklokowska Curie (1867–1934) revolutionized the fields of physics and chemistry with her discovery of the elements radium and polonium. In the field of Physical Cosmology, Henrrietta Swan Leavitt (1868–1911) shares the designation of "parent" with both Albert Einstein and Edwin Hubble. Celebrated for her contributions to being able to calculate the distances among galaxies, discoveries such as universe expansion were made possible. But these women, though they used the scientific method, were not the authors of it and I fear that providing an exhaustive list of the achievements by women serves only to highlight how few are successful in overcoming societal boundaries to make such contributions.

But there is one very interesting woman in history whose work could really only have utilized a form of scientific methodology. Aglaonice of Thessaly, daughter of Hegemon (circa 200 BCE), was known as a sorceress with an uncanny ability to predict the lunar eclipse. No doubt that with careful observation and mathematical calculation making these predictions was as possible as it is

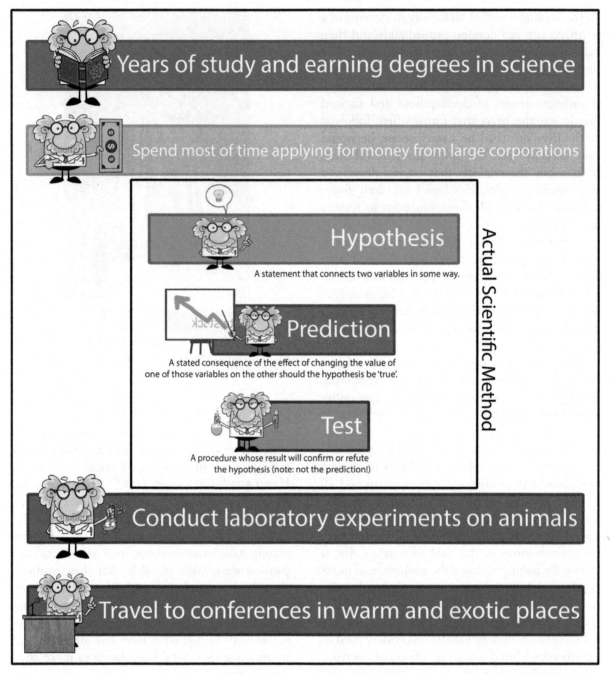

Figure 1.   Though the actual scientific method contains three simple steps and requirements, the perception is that much more is involved and required.

today. It has been suggested that she cultivated her reputation as a sorceress and not as a scientist because there would have been a societal advantage to having others believe her capable of "bringing down the moon".

The term "scientific method" has been used somewhat willy-nilly within this text thus far and it is important to make sure that a clear definition is nailed down here. What do you think of when you read Scientific Method?

No, really. . . . What words come to mind?

For me, the words "simple" and "elegant" are at the front of my mind and the tip of my tongue. It is both of these attributes that have made this methodology one of the most ubiquitous procedural recipes ever devised by humanity. That is a pretty bold statement and certainly the recipe for making bread and many medical procedures are older, but none of these is either simple or elegant though they may also be ubiquitous. What is unfortunate about the reputation of science is that many of us associate it with things that are not part of the method, nor a requirement of the knowledge (Fig 1). The actual scientific method is elegant in its simplicity but also in its design, for with the taking of each small step, the next one becomes easier. So, in essence, writing a hypothesis is the hardest part. And, as you will see, even that is not very hard.

The Scientific Method

If you went to high school in North America you likely learned that the scientific method was a recipe that included anywhere from three to six steps. In its most simplified form and according to the high school curriculum, the scientific method might have looked like this:

1) Hypothesis
2) Prediction
3) Test

So let us begin with this for it is likely to be familiar to you. But as you are reading this, I challenge you to begin to examine why I want to begin here and not end. What is missing from this familiar narrative?

Let's start at the most basic of understandings of the scientific method. A *hypothesis* is a relationship statement between two variables. (It may be that you have learned that it is an "if then" statement or a proposed explanation, or an educated guess. I would ask you to suspend these former learnings for now, or entirely, because they complicate the issue. Indeed, hypotheses *could* be all of

these things, but they are not required according to the definition.) We must keep it simple when writing a hypothesis because we want to be able to pass on smoothly to the next step. So all that is required is to 1) identify two variables, and 2) state that they are related, or that one controls the other. Other than this, a hypothesis has no rules, no template, and no format. For example, perhaps we are interested in undergraduate student performance on final exams. We might want to explore the possible determinants of performance so that we can help our students achieve higher grades. Perhaps we would explore study habits and perhaps we might think that the number of hours that students study has something to do with the grades that they achieve. We therefore have our two variables: 1) number of hours studied, and 2) grade on the exam.

When writing hypotheses, you must demonstrate restraint and only acknowledge that a relationship exists. This is important. Therefore, we use words like "correlated," "caused," "related to," and "affected by" to link the variables. We do not add extra bits of information like possible mechanisms or other influencing variables. This complicates the matter, makes moving on the next step impossible, and could lead you down a blind alley if you end up rejecting the hypothesis because you have done a test to reject the mechanism, even though the actual hypothesis may be supported. In science you take slow, methodical steps. The resulting hypothesis could be:

The final grade that a student receives on an exam is related to the number of hours that he/she studies.

According to our definition of a hypothesis, an equally viable hypothesis could be:

The final grade that a student receives on an exam is related to the odometer reading that each student has on his/her car.

Once we have the hypothesis (let us continue this discussion with the first one), writing out the predictions is pretty easy.

A *prediction* is a description of the nature of the relationship should one of the variables "change." Basically, a prediction suggests a "direction"; it is a prediction of what will happen if you, for example, increase or decrease one of the variables.

If we have the hypothesis:

Hypothesis 1: *The final grade that a student receives on an exam is related to the number of hours that he/she studies.*

Then a prediction arising from that hypothesis could be:

Prediction 1: *The more hours that a student studies, the better he/she will do on the final exam.*

Or

Prediction 2: *The fewer hours that a student studies, the worse that he/she will do on the final exam.*

(Do you see why it is confusing to define a hypothesis as an educated guess, when the above prediction could also be defined as such?)

But! Equally valid would be the following:

Prediction 3: *The fewer hours that a student studies, the better he/she will do on the final exam.*

Here again, we understand further the problem inherent in the definitions that we have been taught previously. A prediction does not have to be logical. It must, as is the case for a hypothesis, only be testable.

What is missing so far? Is a bag full of hypotheses and predictions able to really tell us all things about how the world works? Can we really assemble all of science knowledge using these small bricks of coupled variables?

What's missing from all of this is the humanity. It is the added humanity that allows us to use this basic of concept, the hypothesis, to *seek explanation*.

A *test* is the procedure that you will take in order to figure out if what you predict actually happens. It is therefore a series of steps in itself that depend upon the nature of the predictions, the discipline in which you are working, the resources to which you have access, and more. There is no "one way" of testing a prediction. How can we test whether the number of hours studied affects the grades that students get on their exams? Perhaps a more intriguing question is: will only one test satisfy you that the prediction is "true" or "false" and that the hypothesis is either refuted or accepted? This is where it can get tricky because even if your results are exactly what you predicted, is it possible that you got that result because of some other external influence that was not related to your hypothesis? How many times will you want to run the test, getting the same result, to satisfy yourself that the result is "true"? How many students will you study? There are no concrete answers. Rather, understanding that there are potential weaknesses in your test and working to strengthen as many of them as possible is the best course.

Let us work with the first prediction: *The more hours that a student studies, the better he/she will do on the exam.* What should we do next? How can we test this? We need to design a "fair test." A fair test is a *test where all variables are kept constant except for one.* In this case, the variable that will change will be the number of hours studied. The complication arises when we start to understand that there are very few cases in which *all* the variables can be kept constant between two groups.

If, for example, we were setting up an experiment to test our prediction about hours studying, what would we have to control? The gender of the students? Their ages? Their diets? The courses in which they are enrolled? The grade or year in which they are registered? Some of these are easily kept constant by limiting participation in the study (i.e. grade and course selection), while others are more complicated (i.e. age, gender), and some are impractical (i.e. diet). In other studies, controlling all variables can be easier. Perhaps we can say that it is "easier" to control all the variables in a car crash test, compared to studies on human behaviour, but perhaps this statement only speaks to my

Rather than study what happens to a car when it crashes "in the street," crash tests are designed specifically to eliminate all the confounding variables (i.e. road conditions, traffic, distractors, different obstacles).

ignorance of physics and engineering. Certainly we can appreciate the difference between studying car safety using data collected from 1) traffic accident reports and 2) laboratory crash tests. Traffic accident data represent "real-world" scenarios and incorporate human reaction times but they also contain so many confounding variables including weather conditions, other vehicles, and environmental enrichment. The laboratory data can be strictly controlled and each variable can be analysed separately but it is difficult to apply the conclusions of a small number of tests to real-world scenarios.

How does this apply to figuring out whether the number of hours studied influences the grades that students receive on their exams? We could devise a number of different tests, including:

Test 1: Circulate a survey to all students in all classes in first-year university courses asking them questions related to how many hours they study for each test and the grade that they received.

Test 2: Install small spy-cams into the first-year residence rooms and record how often students are studying for each test. Compare these numbers with their grades on exams.

Test 3: After one exam in one class, circulate a short survey asking students to disclose how many hours they studied for the exam and compare that with the grade that they earned.

Test 4: Divide one class of first-year students into three categories. Group 1 will agree to study for 10 hours, Group 2 for 5 hours, and Group 3 for 1 hour. Compare the grades from each group.

All of these tests would be helpful in addressing the hypothesis and resulting prediction. But which are best scientifically? Which are not possible practically? And will any one test satisfy you to conclude definitively? Take a few minutes to write out the pros and cons associated with each test.

Again, there are no real answers here. However, we can begin to understand the pros and cons of each methodology. This is what really matters and there are a couple of general guidelines. The first one is: if you are going to be inaccurate, be consistently inaccurate. This rule allows us to "get around" the problem of participant observations: where the act of simply observing can have an impact on outcome. Yes, of course, an observer can influence the results, and yes we should work to minimize this impact. But if in the experiment, the observer and the methodology are kept constant then at least we are controlling some of the variation that may occur as a result of inconsistent observation; an imperfect methodology does not mean that it should not be carried out.

The second guideline is that increasing your sample size helps to overcome the influence of confounding variables. The results from a study that involves 20 undergraduate students are likely to be more influenced by confounding variables (such as sex, age, diet) than one that involves 1,000 students.

Once you have carried out your experiments, the data must be analysed and conclusions must be drawn. The analysis portion of the scientific method is beyond the scope of this text but it is a fascinating and equally "grey" topic about which many books have been written.

The conclusions are generally expressed in rather non-committal language. Often we read things like "The data suggest . . .," and "It is likely that. . . ." There is a very specific reason for this: it is usually always possible that a repeat of the experiment will yield contradictory results. (Did you notice that I used the word "usually" here? The first draft of this text did not have this word and, upon reading it over, I realized that I could not state with absolute certainty that there were experiments in which no variation in results had been found.) Following this, we can also use Sir Isaac Newton's four rules of scientific reasoning when trying to interpret results in order to make conclusions:

1) Admit no more causes of natural things than are both true and sufficient to explain their appearances.
2) To the same natural effect, assign the same causes.
3) Qualities of bodies, which are found to belong to all bodies within experiments, are to be esteemed universal.
4) Propositions collected from observation of phenomena should be viewed as accurate or very nearly true until contradicted by other phenomena.

The first rule is now called the Principle of Parsimony, or Occam's Razor. It states that if several explanations are possible, it is the simplest that is probable. For example, in reconciling the movements of the planets, both the geocentric (Earth at the centre of the galaxy) and the heliocentric (Sun at the centre of the galaxy) models are possible but the heliocentric model requires fewer (only seven) assumptions whereas the geocentric model requires many more.

The second rule states that if there is already a reasonable explanation for an observation, then it should be applied to any subsequently identical observations.

Similarly, the third rule states that conclusions reached for an observation should be applied to all cases of that same observation.

Finally, the fourth rule states that once a conclusion has been reached through scientific means, it is to be upheld until proven otherwise.

It is this "until proven otherwise" that is held in high regard within the scientific community and which is often used to describe a fundamental difference between scientific and other forms of knowledge; scientific knowledge is only written in stone until proven otherwise; **a scientist should therefore be willing to accept an alternative explanation for her findings if her initial reasoning is proven false.**

The idea of changing one's mind given convincing evidence is a powerful notion in science. It is why we often talk in terms of probability and wrap our certainties in language of the less certain. It is also science's Achilles Heel; those that seek to attack Science often enter this small culvert in an otherwise fortified wall and say "well, you can never *prove* anything in science, it's all just a *theory.*" While the statement that we can never prove anything is, technically, probably (ha!), correct, we can certainly *disprove* things (a discussion beyond the scope of this text but still fun to think about) and, more importantly, a *scientific theory* is not the same as a theory.

Huh?

A word that is its own antonym is called a contronym: it means itself and its opposite. A case could be made for the word "theory". Other such cases include words like "sanction," "left," and "dust." A theory is commonly defined as "a speculative or conjectural view or idea," whereas a scientific theory is defined as "a well-substantiated explanation of some aspect of the natural world that is acquired through the scientific method and repeatedly tested and confirmed through observation and experimentation." With this definition the "it's only a theory" argument falls flat. In fact, a scientific theory is as sure as scientific knowledge can get; once a group of facts is accepted as theory, there is usually no going back.

Each of these ways of knowing is distinct and important. We have learned that they are distinct in the way in which the knowledge is created, the time at which they played a vital role in our history as humans, and in their consequences, power, and use. Throughout this text we will be looking at knowledge that was created using each of these methods: Traditional, Faith, and Scientific for their invention are intimately tied to the story of the evolution of humanity.

Ecology and Niche
Why Are There So Many Kinds of Animals?*

The Dawn of a New Science

Seeking an explanation about the world around us is a long journey filled with intellectual mysteries and treasures. We, human beings, share this planet with many different species. In fact, the latest estimates are at 8.7 million species, of which only about 1.2 million have been discovered and properly described. Even before any precise estimate could be made, Greek philosophers started to wonder how it is that so many different life forms could even exist.

Aristotle (~300 BC), for instance, proposed that decaying material could be recycled and transformed into living animals by spontaneous action. In essence, the spontaneous generation theory states that life can be generated from different mixtures of inanimate material, where a different recipe will yield different species. For instance, Aristotle observed:

"Other insects are not derived from living parentage, but are generated spontaneously: some out of dew falling on leaves, ordinarily in spring-time, but not seldom in winter when there has been a stretch of fair weather and southerly winds; others grow in decaying mud or dung; others in timber, green or dry; some in the hair of animals; some in the flesh of animals; some in excrements: and some from excrement after it has been voided,

Aristotle thought that life was generated from recycled life material.

Think about it . . .

Take a moment to reflect upon an explanation that you are familiar with that describes how life, as we know it, came to be. Write out a short description here:

_____
_____
_____
_____
_____
_____

---

* Title borrowed from the famous Homage to Santa Rosalia (Hutchinson 1959)

and some from excrement yet within the living animal, like the helminthes or intestinal worms."

As surprisingly as it might sound, scientists generally accepted spontaneous generation as one of the main mechanisms of new life form creation, until Louis Pasteur's famous microbiology experiments in the middle of the 19th century that lead to the discovery, among others, of the rabies vaccine. Together, Louis Pasteur's and Charles Darwin's seminal works brought the final blows to spontaneous generation theories. In particular, Charles Darwin initiated one of the most significant scientific revolutions in modern times when he proposed that new life forms were created through the process of evolution.

Before we move on, can you think of a way to investigate the likelihood of spontaneous generation using the scientific method? (See Practice Assignment)

> Hypothesis: Life can develop from non-living material such as broth.
> Prediction: Sterilized and sealed flasks of broth will have just as much bacteria growing in them than a flask that is sterilized but not sealed.

Louis Pasteur tested this prediction by having three types of flasks, all of them containing sterilized broth: 1) sealed, 2) open, 3) a flask with a curved neck to allow anything "entering" to settle on the bottom of the curve before reaching the broth.

Given your experience, which flask(s) would you predict to have bacteria growing in it (them) after a considerable period of time? When Pasteur observed the bacterial growth in the flasks, he found that only the flask that was open to the air contained bacteria.

In 1668, Francesco Redi, an Italian physician and naturalist, conducted a similar experiment to investigate further the possibility of spontaneous generation. Instead of flasks and broth, Redi used pieces of meat, jars, and cheese cloth. Take a few moments and see if you can reconstruct

Louis Pasteur (1822–1895) performed experiments to disprove Aristotle's spontaneous generation hypothesis.

this experiment to test the hypothesis: life can develop from non-living materials such as meat. First write out a prediction, then design the experiment. And instead of bacteria, let's look for maggots!

Once it was understood that spontaneous generation was not the correct path to follow to understand the diversity of life, there formed a bifurcation among scientists. The science of evolution seeks to understand the processes behind new species generation (i.e.

Malthus' prediction, though unrealistic, certainly resonates today among those people who do not have access to the same resources as others.

Practice Assignment-Fill out and submit this assignment during the first week of class to 1) ensure that you understand the submission procedures and 2) receive feedback on your approach to completing the assignment. This will help you with all assessed assignments in the future. There is no grade associated with this assignment.

Name: _____   Student Number: _____

Design a scientific experiment that will help us to answer the question: is spontaneous generation possible? Make sure that it isn't identical to the one described in the following text.

_____

_____

_____

_____

_____

_____

_____

_____

_____

_____

_____

_____

_____

_____

_____

_____

_____

_____

_____

_____

_____

_____

Marking:

1) Would this experiment help determine whether spontaneous generation is possible?

speciation), and thus from this point, coinciding with the publication of the famous "On the origin of species" from Charles Darwin (1859), evolutionist explorers went on their own journey. On a parallel route to the evolutionists, emerged the ecologist with questions related to, not the existence of diversity over time, but, rather, the co-existence of such great biodiversity. How can millions of species co-exist together when they are limited by both space and resource availability?

Thomas Robert Malthus, a famous political scientist and demographer, had already noted in 1798 that human population growths constantly exceed resource renewal rates. Later, Charles Darwin, inspired by Malthus' calculations, observed:

> "At the former rate, the present population [1871] of the United States (thirty millions), would in 657 years cover the whole terraqueous globe so thickly, that four men would have to stand on each square yard of surface."

This absurd but powerful demonstration illustrates well that without some minimal underlying regulating mechanisms, the co-existence of 8.7 million species on the same relatively small and enclosed planet would be simply impossible.

It is in this historical context that pressing practical issues related to industrialization, increasing population growth, resource depletion, pest and disease outbreaks, and fundamental questions related to species diversity and co-existence, that the field of ecology was created at the end of the 19th century. Ecology, originally defined as the comprehensive science of the relationship of the organism to the environment, borrowing information from well-established sciences like economics, taxonomy, and biology, was about to become one of the most integrative and influential fields of research along the never-ending journey to explain the inner workings of our surrounding environment.

"An Idea That Took a Century to Be Born"* (Hardin 1960)

While evolutionary biologists try to understand the mechanisms leading to the incredible variation of life forms that surround us, ecologists try to understand how living organisms interact among each other and their environment and how they manage to co-exist. Why, for example, are there only 10 species in 1 pond, but 50 in another? Are there some species that always co-occur or that never occur together? Why?

Competitive exclusion is a principle that describes when two species cannot co-exist. An example of this is that of the grey (left) and red (right) squirrels in Britain; their ranges do not overlap.

The discovery of new scientific knowledge often begins with very casual observations that are later linked to theoretical models or experimental results. In 1904, Joseph Grinnell, a keen ornithologist and part-time explorer who began his career when searching for gold during the Klondike gold rush, observed that:

"Two species [of birds] of approximately the same food habits are not likely to remain long evenly balanced in numbers in the same region. One will crowd out the other"

In other words, Grinnell made the observation that two species sharing resources in the same habitat do not get along very well, and usually one will push the other out. Among Grinnell's important contributions to ecology, this statement went mainly unnoticed by the scientific community. However, as we shall see, this seemingly trivial observation will give Grinnell the intellectual claim on a foundational concept of ecology.

In 1934, a Russian ecologist named Georgy Gause published the results of a laboratory experiment that would haunt ecologists for the remainder of the 20th century. Gause, inspired by previous mathematical models of competitive interactions among species, was trying to understand if and how species competing for resources could co-exist in the same habitat. Being a proponent of the reductionist approach to science, he conducted his experiment by simply growing two *Paramecium** species alone or together in small laboratory tubes. Paramecia are interesting unicellular water organisms that feed on bacteria. For his first set of experiments, Gause fed the paramecia with a single species of bacteria. He also made sure that all other environmental conditions (e.g. water temperature and pH) were maintained constant. Then, he simply recorded the population size of each species over time.

When growing each species of paramecium in separate cultures, their respective population size followed the expected quick density increase owing to high bacteria resource availability until the population reached its maximal density when resources (in this case, food) became too scarce because of high competition among individuals. However, in the second set of experiments, when growing the two species together, the same one would always go extinct after a few days.

Gause's results confirmed Grinnell's observation that two species sharing the same resource cannot co-exist in the same habitat. Unfortunately, Gause did not offer any plausible mechanisms or general conclusion about this specific experiment to explain the implications of his results for species co-existence.

It took more than 10 years before another ornithologist, David Lack, working on the finches from Galapagos Islands, offered a mechanistic interpretation of Gause's results:

" My views have now completely changed, through appreciating the force of Gause's contention that two species with similar ecology cannot live in the same region. […] If two species of birds occur together in the same habitat in the same region, eat the same types of food and have the same other ecological requirements, then they should compete with each other, and since the chance of their being equally well adapted is negligible, one of them should eliminate the other completely."

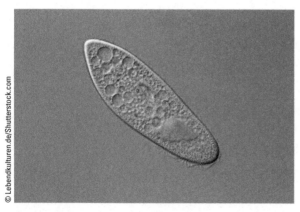

Paramecium caudatum, one of the species used by Gause to demonstrate the principle of competitive exclusion.

The concept referred to by Dr. Lack, and later named the "competitive exclusion principle,"

Assignment 1: Graphing it out.

Name: _____   Student Number: _____

Can you graphically represent the experimental results that Gause observed? (If you need a bit of a refresher on how to make graphs, check out: http://www.wikihow.com/Make-a-Line-Graph). Make sure to label your axes!

First set of experiments:

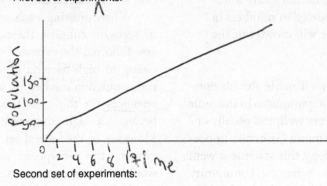

Second set of experiments:

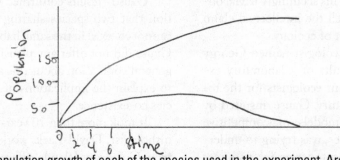

1) Describe the population growth of each of the species used in the experiment. Are they the same in separate cultures?

_____

_____

2) Do any of the population growth curves 'plateau'? Why? or why not?

_____

_____

Marking:

1) Do the graphs match the experimental results?

2) Are the graphs described fully and accurately?

is based on the very fundamental "axiom of inequality": because no two things or processes are ever precisely equal. In the long term, any two entities in competition for the same resource will end up with only one victor. For instance, if two merchants are competing to sell the same product, the most obvious way one merchant will increase its number of customers is by reducing its price. The other merchant's only option (or is it the only option?) is to reduce the price further. This price war will eventually lead to only one winner: the merchant with the highest savings. Note that the difference between the two merchants' wealth is irrelevant; even the slightest little difference of a few dollars will give, over time, only one victorious merchant. The same can be said for species. If two species are competing for the same resource in the same habitat, the slightest difference in their resource acquisition rate will lead to higher reproductive rate by one species that will eventually push the weak competitor to extinction. The competitive exclusion principle with its deep roots in economic and ecological theory took close to a century to be clearly formulated (attributed to Garrett Hardin in 1960). The idea is built on rock hard conceptual logic, and experimental and empirical demonstrations, and it did have important impacts on economic, social, evolution, and ecology science developments. Interestingly, however, the competitive exclusion principle would shed light on one of the greatest scientific paradoxes (see the paradox of the plankton).

Sharing the Pie; More to a Few or Less to Everyone?

Let us come back to our merchants' example (from the previous part). We first assumed that a price war was inevitable because it is obvious that for the exact same product customers will usually buy at the cheapest price. However, when faced with bankruptcy, a merchant would be wisely advised to avoid competition altogether, perhaps by selling another product, with no competitors. Based on this example and following the "inequality axiom,"

if competition for a limited resource is intense, only two outcomes are possible:

1) Competitive exclusion
2) Resource partitioning.

"Resource partitioning" refers quite literally to the separation of the resource pie among the competitors so that they do not compete for the same piece anymore.

One of the earliest examples of this phenomenon in natural systems comes from Robert MacArthur's doctorate dissertation work (1958). Dr. MacArthur was studying a community of five warbler bird species with almost identical requirements in terms of resource and habitat. All five species feed on the same insects, on the same spruce trees. Based on Grinnell's observations and Gause's experiments, these species should not be able to persist in the same habitat, but they did. This is a curious case of observation contradicting well-established theoretical predictions, which has since become legend in ecology. It suggests that more study of these birds is necessary to 1) correct the theoretical model or to 2) complete inadequate observations. To solve this problem, Dr. MacArthur sat in the forest with a pair of binoculars and meticulously observed the behaviour of these five warbler species. Every time a bird went to a tree and ate, he would note the position of the bird, along with many other behavioural observations.

After many exhaustive hours of observation he noticed that on average, each species fed on different parts of the tree and by doing so were avoiding competition for the same space or individual insects. Without such patience by Dr. MacArthur, it would have been impossible to establish that the theory was not wrong, but instead, observations were inadequate.

The warblers example is a case of spatial partitioning of the same resource. Resource partitioning, however, can also occur in time. For instance, two plant species competing for the same essential pollinators could ease competition by flowering at different times of the year (temporal partitioning). Resource partitioning can even sometimes involve morphological differentiation, like a change in root

© Paul Reeves Photography/Shutterstock.com, © Al Mueller/Shutterstock.com

Five warbler species (Left to right: Blackburnian warbler, Cape May warbler, Bay-breasted warbler, Black-throated green warbler, Myrtle warbler) feeding on the same resource but on different parts of the tree to avoid direct competition.

depth to avoid competition for nutrients, or a change to bird's bill shapes to specialize on different seeds.

Of course, one individual of a species cannot go against its own physiological limits and change its root depth, reproductive cycle, or bill shape at will. These changes require changes in genetic expression, and usually take more than one generation to occur (except in some specific cases – see evolution chapter). This is where evolution meets ecology. If two species are very similar and competition is fierce, evolution processes will generally favour changes that will ease competition.

Though evolutionary changes are often directly involved in resource partitioning, it need not be the case. For instance, resource partitioning in space, like in the warblers' case, is easily explained by competitive exclusion itself. Each bird species could potentially feed anywhere on the spruce tree when the other species are not present; however, each species is a better competitor for its own feeding location and therefore can push the other species out. The location of each warbler species on the tree is therefore not caused by fundamental physiological limitations, but rather it is the presence of the other species that set the limits to where each species can be.

The Niche

Dr. MacArthur's work on warblers proposed resource partitioning as a viable mechanism to understand species co-existence. The main challenge from there was to build a coherent generalizable conceptual framework to predict when and how different species can co-exist together. Dr. Evelyn Hutchinson, MacArthur's famous supervisor, was

© Hhelene/Shutterstock.com

Balanus balanoides, a species of barnacle, is almost never found to overlap with *Chthamalus stellatus*.

the first one to put all the pieces together in 1957 and to give birth to what is now known as the Hutchinsonian niche concept.

The best way to understand the niche concept is to turn our attention to the barnacle community of Millport (Scotland) made famous by the keen observations of Dr. Connell, around 1961. Dr. Connell observed that *Chthamalus stellatus* and *Balanus balanoides*, two barnacle species, are never present on the same part of the rocky shore. Instead, *Chthamalus* is almost always found in the highest part, where it is almost never in contact with water, while *Balanus* is only found in the lower part where waves often submerge them. Clean-cut delineations in nature always catch the eyes of good observers and Dr. Connell was curious about this clear spatial demarcation between two similar barnacle species. He performed a series of experiments where he moved *Chthamalus* individuals lower, and *Balanus* individuals higher on the shore. In both cases, he made sure that no individuals of the other species were close enough to interact with the newly transplanted barnacles. Interestingly, he found that *Chthamalus* could survive quite well everywhere on the shore, whereas *Balanus* mortality increased a lot in the upper, drier areas. It turned out that *Balanus* does not tolerate heat and desiccation very well. On the other hand, *Chthamalus* is more tolerant to desiccation and water immersion and thus can thrive anywhere on the intertidal zone. This experiment explained satisfyingly well why no *Balanus* are found higher on the intertidal zone (physical constraints); however, it suggests that *Chthamalus* could potentially be found everywhere, which does not correspond to observations!

In a second part of the same experiment, Dr. Connell moved individuals of *Chthamalus* in the lower part of the shore, but this time he made sure that *Balanus* individuals were close enough to interact with the newly transplanted *Chthamalus* barnacles. In almost each case, *Chthamalus* was overcrowded by *Balanus* and totally excluded from the lower zone. The key element here is that barnacles are sessile organisms (they cannot get up and move around) that tightly fix themselves to stones (to resist wave action!). Space is therefore limiting for barnacles because there is only

a certain amount of space that a stone can provide. *Chthamalus* can survive very well closer to the shoreline without *Balanus*; however, *Balanus* reproduce quicker, and so it is only a question of time before space becomes an issue and *Balanus* "smothers, undercuts or crushes the *Chthamalus*" (Connell, 1961). The spatial partition of the habitat between the two species in this case is caused by both the physiological limitations of *Balanus*, which prevent this species from reaching the upper limit of the shore to overcrowd and exclude *Chthamalus*, and by the competitive exclusion of *Chthamalus* from the lower part of the shore.

In MacArthur's warbler experiment, there was no evidence for physical limitations on where each bird could be on the tree. Here, *Balanus* barnacles cannot survive in the highest parts of the shore. These physiological limitations to environmental conditions constitute fundamental constraints to where *Balanus* and *Chthamalus* barnacles can be. In the absence of each other's presence, *Chtamalus* would live happily everywhere while *Balanus* would be limited to the lowermost parts. If you draw the potential distribution of *Balanus* and *Chtamalus* on the shore based only

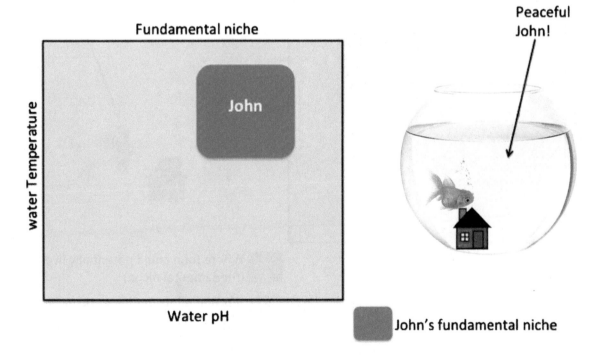

on environmental limitations, the result would correspond to what Dr. Hutchinson referred to as the "fundamental niche" (see the Figure below). It corresponds to where a species could potentially grow and reproduce if it would be alone in the universe (i.e. no interactions of any kind with other species). Now, if you draw the distribution of *Balanus* and *Chtamalus* when they have to share the same space, the result would correspond to what Dr. Hutchinson referred to as the "realized niche" (see the Figure below). Among all the different environmental conditions where a species can potentially survive ("fundamental niche"), the species can actually only occur in a portion of its fundamental niche because of interactions with other species (realized niche).

Okay…What Is Niche?! – The Tale of Peaceful John

The niche concept can be hard to grasp because it is nothing but an abstraction: it is not a habitat, or a physical place of any sort. Rather, the niche of a species is built by all the environmental conditions and species interactions that affect its growth and reproduction, and therefore, as a consequence, limit where it can "be." If you were to draw a graph of the effects of all the variables that can affect a species survival, the niche would correspond to the space in the graph where this species can positively grow and reproduce: where it can survive.

When thinking about the required conditions for a species to be present in a specific location, Dr. Hutchinson first started by thinking about the surrounding environment of a particular species. Indeed, a species, a goldfish in an aquarium perhaps, can only live, grow, and reproduce within a certain range of environmental conditions. In the figure you see that your goldfish is only happy within certain limits of water temperature and pH. This is what Hutchinson called the "fundamental" niche of the species – i.e. if you imagine all the possible sets of environmental conditions that could affect your goldfish, put them on a graph with as many axes as there are conditions:

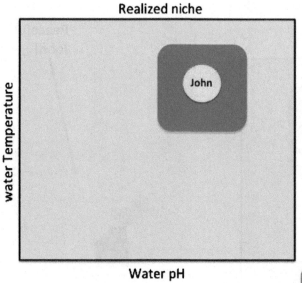

Realized niche

water Temperature

Water pH

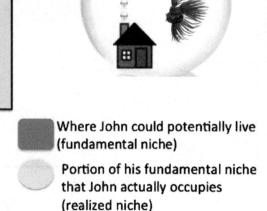

Bad ass fish!

Where John could potentially live (fundamental niche)

Portion of his fundamental niche that John actually occupies (realized niche)

Assignment 2: Draw it out.

Name: _____ Student Number: _____

Using the story of the barnacles, can you illustrate the concepts of Fundamental and Realized Niche? Below is a diagram of a tidal zone. Draw the two species of barnacles on the tidal zone and identify their fundamental and realized niche. Label everything that you can to ensure that another person can understand your drawing. (Hint: read on just a little bit further for a discussion of the different kinds of niches.)

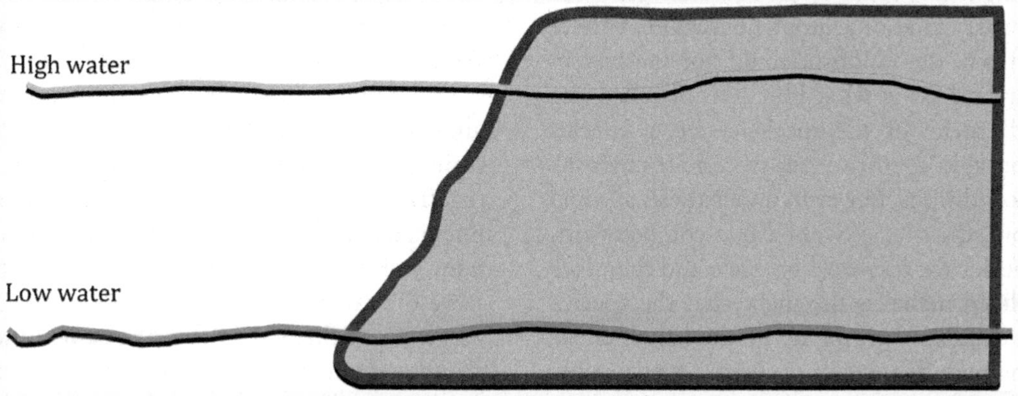

High water

Low water

Is the fundamental niche always larger than the realized niche? Can you think of any scenarios where it could be the opposite?

_____

_____

_____

_____

_____

_____

_____

_____

_____

_____

_____

Marking:

1) Does the drawing represent the observation of the barnacle niches?

2) Is the answer to the question insightful and interesting?

where would your fish be able to thrive on this graph? You just found the fundamental niche of your fish, congrats! (Definitely avoid telling your uncle about it at a holiday dinner!)

Now, of course, no species lives alone in a vacuum. Species constantly have to interact with other species. Imagine that you introduce another fish in your aquarium. This new fish is not a nice peaceful fish but instead a species that wants to occupy the whole space of the aquarium for himself, the nasty kind of grumpy housemate. Where do you think the goldfish would go? (answer in the figure!). This is what Hutchinson called the "realized" niche of the species – i.e. a species might be able to thrive under certain environmental conditions, but even under these optimal conditions, the species will have to compete with other species for resources or space and therefore the "realized niche" is the niche that the species actually occupies, within its fundamental niche, when you include interactions with other species.

The Functional Niche Concept (Eltonian Niche—"What the Species Does")

Even before MacArthur's work and the Hutchinsonian's niche concept, another English ecologist had already suggested a very different approach to the niche concept in his seminal book "Animal Ecology" (1927):

> "When an ecologist says 'there goes a badger,' he should include in his thoughts some definite idea of the animal's place in the community to which it belongs, just as if he had said, 'there goes the vicar'."

The functional niche of a species corresponds to "what he does"—producer, herbivore, carnivore, ecosystem engineer (beaver, ants, human!), kind of like professor, president, grandmother etc.

Elton developed his niche concept in an attempt to classify a maze of complexity into simpler boxes. Who you are is not important as long as you accomplish approximately the same

functions, then you are the same. Ecologists often use an Eltonian niche approach when they are studying food webs. By classifying species that eat the same prey into the same "functional" group they can significantly decrease the complexity of the studied system and build general theories about the way food webs work. Indeed, both the Hutchinsonian and Eltonian niche concepts are related to each other. If you think about the Hutchinsonian niche graph (see fish example above), species sharing the same Eltonian niche should in theory be very close to each other.

The functional niche is used to simplify and understand complex systems. Instead of measuring every potential parameter, you just group together species that share the same function. For instance, depending on your research question, you could consider that all police officers serve the same general purpose in our society, so why not put them all within the same functional group regardless of other individual details? Then do the same for every profession, draw all these boxes and add the interactions among them. At the end you will get an impressively accurate, although strongly simplified, representation of the inner working of human societies. From there you could even compare different societies by comparing the different structures among

© Zakharchenko Anna/Shutterstock.com

societies (what boxes or links are different, absent or new) or ask yourself what would happen if all mail delivery people went extinct?

Here we have used human social structure as an analogy, with people of different professions serving different roles and, therefore, having 'different niches'. But an important distinction is required here. A niche describes a role of a species within an ecosystem. It reflects all the interactions that that species has with its environment and the other species living within it. But with humans, it is more of a 'grey' area because yes, as a species, we have a role, but that role varies markedly with geographical range and has changed over time. Perhaps the most important distinction though is that while a profession often describes a role within the human species, the niche describes the role within the entire ecosystem.

The Paradox of the Plankton

One interesting implication of the *competitive exclusion* principle is that in any given habitat, only one species should be found utilizing each resource. However, in natural systems, the number of species found co-existing on a very limited number of resources is often high. This leads to an interesting paradox where we have an accepted principle (competitive exclusion), confirmed by mathematical models, experiments (Gause), and observations (Grinnell and Lack), but according to this same principle the possible number of species on the planet should be much smaller than it is.

Evelyn Hutchinson was puzzled by this question. More specifically, he was wondering how so many species of phytoplankton could be found in one lake:

"The problem that is presented by the phytoplankton is essentially how it is possible for a number of species to co-exist in a relatively isotropic or unstructured environment all competing for the same sorts of materials. [. . .] According to the principle of *competitive exclusion*

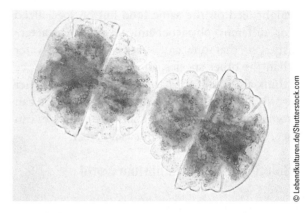

Phytoplankton are microscopic photosynthesizing organisms.

known by many names and developed over a long period of time by many investigators, we should expect that one species alone would outcompete all the others so that in a final equilibrium situation the assemblage would reduce to a population of a single species."

As is the case with most apparent paradoxes in science, the solution usually lies with more detailed observations and the answer is found by the extension or unification of current theories rather than by simply rejecting them. The case of the competitive exclusion principle and how species can co-exist is still not fully resolved in ecology. However, it is interesting to note that most of the plausible solutions to this problem were already envisioned by Dr. Hutchinson as early as 1959.

Solution 1. Undetected resource partitioning

"It's not what you look at that matters, it's what you see"

(Henry David Thoreau)

The most obvious solution is that a habitat for which we see one resource actually contains more than one. A single tree can be perceived as only one resource; however, MacArthur's work has shown that, at least for warblers, it represents many different resources that allow for co-existence. Two algae species in a water tank might feed on the same food but be specialized for different physicochemical water characteristics so that one can survive in deeper water than the other species, allowing for co-existence (think also about the barnacles example). In other words, the difference between two niches can sometimes be much more subtle than the eyes can see, or than our instruments can detect.

Solution 2. Non-equilibrium world

> *"When the wind of change blows, some people build walls, others build windmills"*
>
> (Chinese proverb)

Most mathematical models and experiments assume that competition among species occurs in stable environments where there are no other sources of change. This is a useful simplification that is indeed not representative of most natural systems in constant flux. The two paramecia species in Gause's experiment could co-exist over time if a predator with a preference for the best competitor was introduced, therefore reducing its abundance. A plant with poor competing ability for light would go completely extinct with no fire or wind to open the canopy. The truth is that the natural world very rarely reaches this equilibrium point on which most conceptual models are based. In itself, this dynamic nature of natural systems allows the co-existence of many more species than would be otherwise possible.

Solution 3. The importance of trade-offs

> *"Nothing in life is certain except death, taxes and the second law of thermodynamics"*
>
> (Seth Lloyd)

No living organism can use more energy than they have; this is a trivial rule with utterly important consequences. It means that if you want to be very good at something, you will need to compromise by doing something else less good. If a plant species invests most of its energy into big seeds, then it is very

likely that it would not have many of them, while a plant species investing into quantities will likely have smaller seeds. These trade-offs, whether they are physiological or behavioural, have very important implications for evolution and for ecology. One of these trade-offs is that sometimes they can allow species to co-exist. In the seeds example above, the species with fewer bigger seeds will have a competitive advantage over smaller seeds because it can withstand harsher environmental conditions and can provide more energy for the seedlings to grow. However, bigger seeds do not disperse as easily and as far. Therefore, even if the species with big seeds would competitively exclude the one with smaller seeds when they co-occur, the species with many small seeds can disperse better into new habitats, and therefore escape competition by being always ahead of the dominant competitor. In ecology, this is known as the competition-colonization trade-off, a concept based on the idea that good competitors are often bad disperser and vice-versa. The same might be true of the plankton. Can you think of a scenario applied to plankton that would describe a competition-colonization trade-off?

Conclusion—Why Are There So Many Kinds of Animals?

One could argue that the main question of this chapter, which was first asked many years ago by Evelyn Hutchinson, is filled with imprecisions. First, there is a problem of scale: does the question seek to answer why there are so many different kinds of animals on the entire planet or does it refer to the total number in one location or habitat? Then, there is the problem of defining the proper level of resolution corresponding to a "kind," and if this changes depending on the scale at which we are looking. Fortunately, you should, at this point of the book if not by the end, have the resources necessary to offer potential solutions to these distinct challenges. As for a definitive answer, no one person can pretend to have one and if someone is claiming that they do, ask them what they are selling.

The Building Blocks of Biology

Cells

In the 1600s, after the invention of the microscope, Antonie van Leeuenhoek and Robert Hooke made an amazing discovery. Antonie looked at a sample of pond water under a microscope and found it to be teeming with extremely small life.

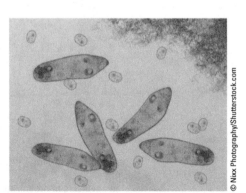

Pond water contains microscopic organisms that play an essential role in the ecosystem. *Daphnia*, the water flea (left), Rotifer (center), and *Paramecium* (right)

When Hooke placed tissue from large living creatures under the microscope, he saw a repeating arrangement of honeycomb-like blocks. Regardless of from where it was taken in the body of an organism or as a single organism living in a pond, these blocks were all surprisingly similar. No matter the type of organism, mammalian or reptilian, insect, plant, microorganism, or otherwise, we are all made of the same building blocks: cells. Before we can understand anything about genetics, evolution, or species, we need to have a firm understanding of this fundamental biological unit.

As the basic structural and functional unit of living things, cells are responsible for all functions throughout a living organism. They are responsible for tasks ranging from their own replication and growth to producing proteins

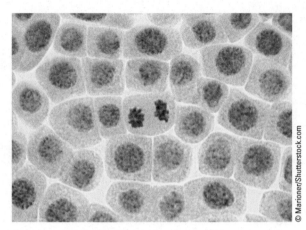

The repeating blocks of living tissue: the cell.

and working together in order to perform tasks necessary for life, such as breathing and digesting food.

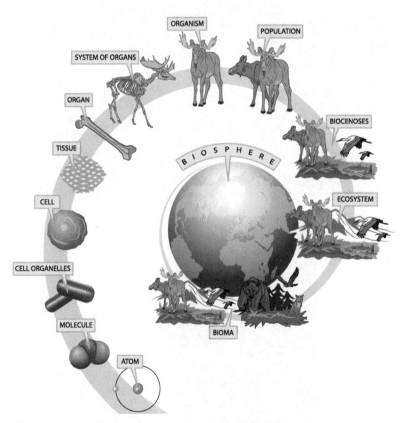

Biological levels of organization: each level is nested within the one above.

In multicellular organisms, similar cells are grouped together in order to form specific tissues. These tissues are part of an organ within an organ system. All of the organ systems together form the structures and functions that are the organism. Are you beginning to pick up on a pattern here? Biological organization is often referred to as a "nested hierarchy"; each group is defined as "a whole bunch of the group below." So, the definition of a "tissue" is "a whole bunch of cells" and the definition of an organ system is "a whole bunch of organs."

Cells may have a variety of appearances, although they all have the same basic components called organelles (therefore, a whole bunch of organelles makes up a cell). Organelles perform tasks necessary for the cell to survive, but cannot survive on their own outside of the cell. These tasks range from producing energy for the cell and transporting items within the cell, to creating

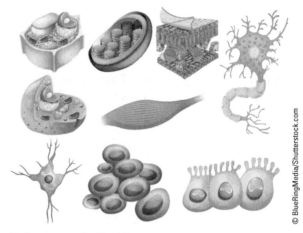

Various types of cells.

proteins that perform functions within the cell or travel to stimulate actions on distant cells. The actions of a variety of different organelles are described in Table 1.

Table 1. The functions of the organelles within eukaryotic cells.

Organelle	Role
Cell membrane	Semipermeable membrane that surrounds a cell, enclosing its contents, provides support, and controls movement of materials in and out of cell
Cell wall	Gives cell more structure and protection, only found in plant cells
Centriole	Organizes the assembly of microtubules during cell division
Chloroplast	Generates sugar from sunlight, only in plant cells
Cytoplasm	Gel-like substance within the cell, supports and protects cell organelles
Endoplasmic reticulum	Carries materials through cell's extensive network of membranes, often a site of protein production
Golgi complex	Responsible for manufacturing, sorting, and exporting cellular products
Lysosomes	Break down old cell parts and larger food stuffs down into smaller pieces
Mitochondrion	Generates energy by breaking down sugars
Nuclear membrane	Controls movement of materials into/out of nucleus
Nucleolus	Is the site of preliminary steps in ribosome creation
Nucleopore	Passages in the nuclear membrane that allow nucleic acids and proteins to move in and out of nucleus
Nucleus	Controls gene expression, replicates, and houses hereditary material (DNA)
Peroxisome	Site of fatty acid breakdown
Ribosome	Responsible for protein assembly
Vacuole	Stores water, food, and metabolic and toxic wastes

Cell Theory

In 1838, two scientists, Matthias Schleiden and Theodor Schwann, combined forces to develop what we call the cell theory. This theory remains largely supported and is based on the following postulates:

1) Cells are the basic structural and functional units of all living organisms

This first postulate became apparent from the dramatic rise of studies conducted on cells that occurred after van Leeuenhoek and Hooke's discoveries. In a fiction-like reality it was found that every living specimen was created of these smaller microscopic living cells that work together to create structure, or complete tasks necessary for life of the whole organism. Although all cells are made of the same components they can have a variety of shapes, specific to the tasks that they perform and area in which they are found. A nerve cell, for example, has a structure that is conducive to detecting and transmitting information, while a cell that lines the stomach has extra surface area to absorb nutrients.

2) Cells are both distinct entities and building blocks of more complex organisms

The microorganisms Antony van Leeuenhoek found are examples of cells with distinct entities. They are completely free living specimens, able to attain their own food and interact with their environment as individual cells. Hooke's discovery on the other hand was of similar cells in extremely close proximity, functioning together to form a part of an entire organism and unable to survive individually.

3) All cells come from pre-existing cells

In the 1800s, the prevailing view was that living organisms spontaneously generated from the assembly of non-living objects. For example, it was thought that maggots arose from dead meat, man from dust, and insects from straw and pond water. There were even recipes to make certain creatures. For example, leaving basil sandwiched between two bricks in the sunlight could make a scorpion, and leaving sweaty underwear with husks of wheat in open-mouthed jars created mice. Along this line of thought Schleiden and Schwann could not piece together from where, exactly, cells arose other than by the self-assembly of non-living materials. This is referred to as spontaneous generation.

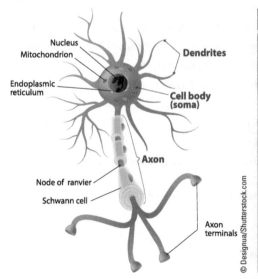

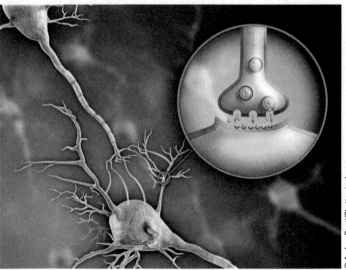

A nerve cell (neuron; left) is structured to meet its function of acquiring and transmitting chemical information (right).

Today, we know that the above examples of spontaneous generation are simply not true. (Unless I am the only one still waiting on my pet scorpion?) Through research we have found that cells duplicate their contents and divide to form multiple cells, which we call daughter cells. These daughter cells will then later duplicate their contents and divide to form into more daughter cells, which will create more daughter cells, and so on. For this reason we have added another postulate to the cell theory:

4) Complete sets of genetic information are replicated and passed on during cell division

Gregor Mendel and Genetics

One of the shortfalls of Darwin's theory of Natural Selection, (that is, the disproportional passing on of the fittest traits in a population given the environmental conditions due to increased rates of reproductive success) at the time that it was proposed was that the exact method of how traits could be passed along from parents to offspring was unknown. Little did Darwin know that the solution to one of his criticisms was answered long before his time. Gregor Johann Mendel was a friar in the region that is now the Czech Republic. After failing his exams to teach biology and natural history, Mendel continued his academic contribution from 1856 to 1866 through independent research on peas. With a strong mathematical background, Gregor Mendel was able to bring a new perspective to inheritance and, by breeding peas, was able to solve the mystery of how inheritance works, sort of.

Before Mendel, we had many ideas about how genetic information was passed on. The various guesses about inheritance ranged from genetic information from both parents mixing together to create traits that are a hybrid of their parents, to the Aristotelian belief that semen formed an embryo from the menstrual blood of women. Unfortunately, Mendel's work went undiscovered for nearly half a century. This was because his mathematical approach to his research made it

difficult to understand and because his research was published in an obscure journal where his work went largely unread.

His work was rediscovered in 1900, resulting in an explosion of inheritance studies and the creation of the branch of biology called genetics. Mendel was posthumously coined as the founder of genetics due to his revolutionary work in discovering the laws of inheritance.

Mendel's research

The pea plant traits that Mendel studied are all quite simple in their mode of expression because they are dichotomous, meaning that there are only two forms of expression of each trait. Mendel monitored seven different traits within the plants, one of them being the colour of the flowers. When crossing white flowering pea plants with red flowering pea plants, in what is called the parent generation, he found that the offspring, the first filial, or F1 generation, consisted of all red plants.

When self-pollinating the F1 red flowering plants, he made the incredible discovery that one-quarter of the resulting generation, the second filial or F2 generation, had white flowers, while the remaining plants were red flowering pea plants. Furthermore, when self-pollinating the F2 generation, the white flowering plants and one-third of the red flowering plants were true breeding, meaning that all following self-pollinated generations created offspring plants with the exact same flower colour as their parent. Self-pollinating the remaining two-thirds of the red flowering pea plants from the F2 generation resulted in the exact same distribution of traits throughout offspring as self-pollinating the red flowering plants from the F1 generation. Confused? Take a few moments to draw it out. Hopefully it will become much clearer.

Now, can you figure out how this could happen? Mendel's solution was that the colour of the plants must be passed down in hereditary units, which we now call genes. To account for the mathematical array of the colours of offspring generations of pea plants, there must be at least two variations of these

Gregor Mendel, the founder of genetics.

units, where one can mask or alter the presence of the other. The different variations of genetic units are what we call alleles. From Mendel's research and the uncovering of the coding of inheritance, or genes and alleles, we were able to create the three laws of inheritance: the Law of Dominance, the Law of Segregation, and the Law of Independent Assortment.

The law of dominance

Now here is where it can get tricky. To display two different colours there must be two alleles (of the same gene) that can control colour. After much deliberation Mendel decided that one allele must be dominant over the other, masking the presence of the other allele from being outwardly expressed. (Remember, we inherit half of our DNA from our mother and half from our father, just like plants do!) In the case of the pea plant flower colours in the parent generation, where a white flowering pea plant was crossed with a red one, the offspring were all red. Given

that the offspring had equal genetic contribution from both of their parents, the red colouration masked the white colouration. We know that the white colouration must still have been somehow present as it appeared in the offspring of all of the F1 generation when they were self-pollinated. In genetics nomenclature, this would mean that the allele for the red colouration is dominant, whereas the allele for the white flower colouration is recessive. To display the genes present for a trait, or the genotype of the trait, we use a single letter. The genotype is the composition of the genes, consisting of either dominant or recessive alleles, or a combination of both. Since there are two alleles for the flower colour trait, this means that there are two letters that represent the single gene. The white flower, being recessive, would be given the small letter abbreviation. For this example, let us use the letter "a" to signify flower colour and give the white flower the nomenclature "aa." Since the red gene is dominant it is expressed with a capital letter. If the red flower is true breeding it would have the genotype "AA," and the individual red flowered plants that carry the white gene are called heterozygous, meaning they have both a recessive "a" and dominant "A." Their genotype can be written as either "aA" or "Aa." In genetics, if an individual displays the dominant trait but we do not know which alleles are present, we will often abbreviate the genetic structure "A-." Makes sense right? Since we do not know the entire genetic make-up of the individual, if it displays the dominant trait we can safely deduce that it has at least one of the dominant alleles.

The physical or outward appearance of the genotype is called the phenotype (think **phy**sical **ph**enotype; **gen**es **gen**otype). In our example of pea plant flower colours, the phenotype of white flowers has a genotype of aa, whereas the phenotype of having red flowers has the genotype AA, Aa, or aA. Any feature, character, or trait that you can imagine is called the phenotype, and it can be controlled by a multitude of genes that make up the genotype for that feature.

This dominance scheme, where the dominant trait is always expressed, is called simple dominance. Life can, of course, get more complicated than that. There are exceptions from the Law of Dominance, such as codominance, where heterozygous individuals express an intermediate of both the dominant and recessive traits, making the traits neither dominant nor recessive but of equal strength. An example of this is in snapdragons where the offspring of snapdragons with red flowers crossed with those with white flowers create hybrids, or individuals heterozygous for the flower colour gene, with pink flowers.

There is also sex-linked dominance where the dominant and recessive properties of the genes are based on the gender of the individual that has the gene. A fantastic and famous example of this is baldness in humans. In men, the gene controlling baldness is inherited as dominant, whereas in women the baldness gene takes on a recessive role. This means women must receive two genes coding for baldness in order to go bald, whereas men only need to receive the baldness gene from one parent. There is a wealth of other gene dominance types ranging from multiple genes controlling a single trait to environmental factors influencing the expression of a gene. The Law of Dominance is simply the expression of dominant traits over recessive ones. It states that whenever a dominant allele is present, it will mask over the presence of the recessive one. Of course, as with Mendel's Laws of Segregation and Independent Assortment, this is not always the case.

The law of segregation

In Mendel's pea plant experiment, as well as with most if not all reproduction, each offspring receives a single allele from each parent. With Mendel's parent generation peas, the white flowered parent plant passed on the recessive "a-" or "-a" allele, and from the other parent the offspring received either the "-A" or the "A-." When egg and sperm, collectively known as gametes, are made, the genes separate so that reproductive cells have only half of the genetic material of their owner. This means that when the egg and the sperm come together, they bring half the genetic material from their respective owner to combine and have enough genetic material to create an entirely new individual. This separation of alleles occurs during the creation of gametes so that offspring have only one complete gene for each trait, and is called the Law of Segregation. The Law of Segregation means that every individual contains a pair of alleles for each particular trait. When any individual produces gametes, the copies of a gene separate so that each gamete receives only one allele, or one copy of the gene.

This means that heterozygous individuals, or individuals that have both dominant and recessive alleles for a trait, are capable of passing either the dominant or the recessive allele on to their offspring. As mentioned with Mendel's Law of Dominance, there are exceptions to each of Mendel's laws. In the case of the Law of Segregation, sometimes mistakes occur, and the genes of the parents, which are located on complex cross like structures of DNA called chromosomes, do not fully separate. Often times this can result in failure of the foetus to reach full term, or if the offspring is born then there can be a range of further medical complications. In extreme cases, such as Klinefelter syndrome, instead of passing on a single chromosome, one parent passes on two chromosomes. This creates a duplication of many genes and results in a sterile male.

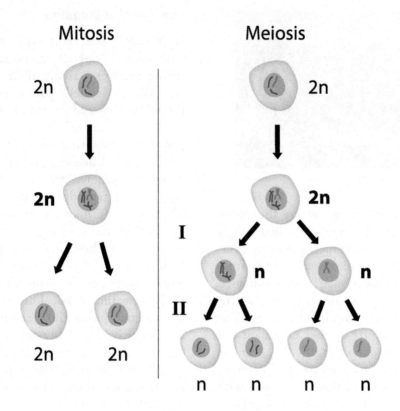

Mitosis

2n

2n

2n   2n

Meiosis

2n

2n

I

n   n

II

n   n   n   n

The Law of Segregation, where genes separate so that only one allele from each parent will be passed on to the offspring.

The law of independent assortment

Mendel researched not only the inheritance of the colour of pea plant flowers, but also the inheritance of the location of the flower, shape, and coat tint of the seed, the shape of the pod and unripe pod colour, as well as the height of the mature plant. Over the course of 7 years Mendel raised and tested over 29,000 pea plants. Having done so many crosses he was able to thoroughly assess if the presence of one trait was linked to another. As such, he drew the conclusion that traits were not linked. The location of the flower had no impact on its seed shape, just as every other trait had no effect on the presence of any other trait on the plant. For this reason the Law of Independent Assortment was derived from Mendel's work. The Law of Independent Assortment means that the alleles that are passed on for one gene have no relation or impact on which alleles are passed on for another gene.

> **Did you know . . .**
>
> All of your chromosomes are identical between each cell (with the exception of gametes as they only have half of your genetic information and red blood cells that carry no genetic information). Genes are made of two alleles, which have a particular place or loci within your DNA. Your DNA is intricately folded up and looped around to make chromosomes. All your chromosomes, 23 pairs or 46 chromosomes, make up your genome.

Punnet squares

The chances of a certain trait appearing in an offspring can be calculated using something called a Punnet square. With a Punnet square for a single gene you put the alleles of the one parent across one side of a 2×2 square, and the alleles of the other parent go along the adjacent side. The four boxes within the square represent the four possible

Pp   **X**   Pp

X	P	p
P		
p		

Punnet Square

X	P	p
P	PP	pP
p	Pp	pp

Genotypes of offspring

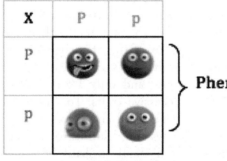

Phenotypes of offspring

Images © Shutterstock.com

The creation of a Punnet square based on the crossing of two hybrid blue monsters. As per the Law of Segregation, each monster will pass on only one of its alleles onto each of the offspring. For this reason, the alleles for each gene are separated and placed at the top or the side of the Punnet square. The row or column adjacent to the alleles is then filled with the respective parent allele. Once the square has been filled, the potential genotypes of the offspring can be seen. Based on this cross of two hybrid monsters, 25% of the offspring will be homozygous dominant, 25% of the offspring will be homozygous recessive, and 50% of the offspring will be heterozygous. The phenotypes of the offspring will be that 75% of the offspring will have the dominant trait, or the blue fur, and 25% will have the recessive pink fur.

gene combinations in the offspring that can be expressed based on their parents' genes. Based on Mendel's Law of Independent Assortment, the genes from each parent have an equal likelihood of being passed on to the offspring, as such alleles that are placed on either side of the box are transferred to the row or column that they are in front of. Since there are four outcomes that are equally likely of being created, each of the boxes represents a genotype that has a 25% chance of occurring. The Punnet square tells you the genotype of the offspring, and from the genotype you can determine what the phenotype would be. For instance, in a hypothetical situation where blue-haired creatures "PP" (therefore blue is dominant) and pink-haired creatures "pp" (therefore pink is recessive) have created a bunch of blue offspring, all with the genes "Pp." By an unfortunate chance, two blue offspring with the genes "Pp" procreate and we want to know the chances of the offspring's genotype being purely dominant blue alleles, or a homozygous dominant genotype, "PP," being a mix of blue and pink alleles "Pp," which is also called heterozygous, of having only the recessive gene "pp," otherwise known as homozygous recessive.

If we were to fill out a Punnet square we would then find that there is a 25% chance of the offspring being homozygous dominant (PP), a 25% chance of the offspring being homozygous recessive (pp), and a 50% chance a heterozygous offspring (Pp or pP). If we wanted to determine the phenotype of the offspring, we would know that any of the offspring with a dominant gene would display the dominant trait, which in this case is the blue hair colour. When looking at the Punnet square we would find that three of the offspring squares have a dominant gene within it. This means that ¾ or 75% of the offspring would be blue, whereas 25% would be pink.

As mentioned earlier, separate genes for separate traits are passed independently of one another from parents to offspring. Alleles of different genes passed on to the offspring have nothing to do with the selection of a gene for any other trait. This is why, when crossing two hybrids, or heterozygous individuals, Mendel

This Punnet square is the result of a dihybrid cross, meaning both parents are heterozygous for both traits of interest. Instead of having only two possible combinations of alleles to pass to their offspring, as per the Law of Independent Assortment, there are now four different possibilities of allele combinations to pass on. In turn, this results in 16 different genotypes and 4 different phenotypes. The phenotypes are represented by the colour of the squares. Individuals that display the dominant phenotypes for both traits are blue, for only the first trait are green, only the second trait are orange, and those that are recessive for both traits are purple.

always got the phenotypic result of 3 dominant:1 recessive in the offspring. In a dihybrid Punnet square, when you look at a cross between two individuals or self-pollination where the individuals or individual is heterozygous for two separate genes, the resulting phenotypic spread is 9:3:3:1. In this case, 9/16 of the offspring display the dominant phenotype for both traits, 3/16 of the offspring display only 1 dominant trait, and 3/16 display only the other dominant trait, and only 1/16 of offspring only express recessive traits. To create a Punnet square for a dihybrid cross, you simply have to add more rows and columns to account for the additional and equally probable combinations of genes that can be passed on. One alteration is that there are now 16 different genotypes and 4 phenotypes that can be created, which must be accounted for if you are attempting to produce the probabilities of each genotype or phenotype.

Genetic information is the instruction manual for how a cell should operate. For future cells to survive and go on to divide, they must be able to pass these instructions on to future cells. The molecule that contains the genetic information and is an integral part of cell division is deoxyribose nucleic acid. You will likely recognize it by its abbreviation

DNA. The discovery of DNA and its function was a key to many questions. It is how hereditary information is passed on from parents to offspring, and it provides the code that creates proteins, which are the most important molecules of life. It tells cells what to produce and when, how to interact with other cells, and how to duplicate. To top it all off, it is scrunched down to a near-unimaginable size, thanks to specialized proteins that organize DNA strands into complex structures of coils and loops. DNA is not only the manual for how a cell should operate, but it is also the manual for the structure and organization of multicellular organisms. It is the manual that makes a dog a dog, a fly a fly, a tree a tree, and you, you.

> **Did you know . . .**
> Each single cell in the human body contains approximately 2 m of DNA stored within the cell's nucleus, which is an organelle that is 0.000006 m wide. This is equivalent to fitting 40 km of thread into a tennis ball!

DNA Structure

In 1953, three very famous scientists, Maurice Wilkins, James Watson, and Francis Crick, were able to determine the structure of DNA by making large three-dimensional models of potential DNA structures. DNA is a long strand of molecules connected together in a ladder-like structure. Each half of the ladder contains a string of four possible "letters" to create one really long "word." Though there is some variation in this calculation, it is thought that if you were to stretch out the DNA of a human cell, it would be about 2 m long. This "little" molecule is a complex computer with astounding simplicity in its design. The four possible "letters", called nucleotides, are actually paired: purine A (adenine) always pairs with pyrimidine T (thymine) and pyrimidine C (cytosine) always pairs with purine G (guanine). And it is this simple fact that makes DNA remarkable. When the DNA molecule is "unzipped," each side consists of a template for the opposite side's complementary letters.

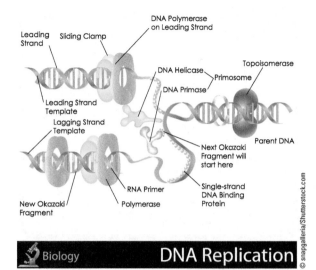

Biology **DNA Replication**

So if the one side reads ACG, the following string is required to make up the missing side: TGC. On the side of the nucleotides where the purine and pyrimidines, or ladder rungs, do not connect the nucleotides, they are attached to a sugar called deoxyribose. The deoxyribose molecules are further connected to each other by phosphates. These sugars and phosphates are bonded in sequence forming the sides or backbone of the helical ladder.

The backbones of the ladder are pieced together in a direction-specific manner when they are created. This causes the backbones of the fully formed DNA helix to have directionality, each side running in opposite directions of the other. Amazingly, the DNA in each cell of a multicellular organism is the exact same. What separates the cells into different structures and functions of the organism are which part of the genome is being expressed. The entirety of DNA within a cell is called the genome. Specific segments of the DNA, are called genes and are used to make proteins.

DNA is not just about replicating itself; it also provides the blueprint for protein. And though it may sound like a minor function, "living" is all about protein production. Here is how all of that works:

We mentioned before that DNA can unzip itself so that each strand can be copied on the complementary strand. With protein synthesis, instead of a complementary strand of DNA

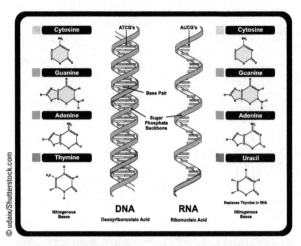

DNA and RNA are made up of four base pairs called "letters." They are the same in each molecule except for thymine and uracil.

being assembled and then fixed along each side, a ribonucleic acid (RNA) strand is assembled. RNA also has these complementary bases with the minor exception of T, which is replaced by U (uracil). The RNA then moves out of the center of the cell, called the nucleus, and the DNA molecule zips up. But why is there this extra step? RNA, at first glance, may appear to be a waste of energy. And it is not uncommon to find "wastes" in nature. (On a side note, nature does not optimize much.) In many cases, achieving optimum may take too much energy or may not be appropriate in light of the environment (e.g. specializing on an energy-rich food source may first seem to be the best strategy but the generalist strategy that evolves is one in the context of competition for resources and resilience to environmental change). RNA may seem to be a bit of a waste but think about the importance of the DNA molecules. They must be preserved and protected. The nucleus serves that function. But if all of the proteins are being assembled and moved out of the nucleus, there is the potential for damage. It is better to send the message, or the blueprint, out of the nucleus where the proteins can be assembled without risk to the DNA.

With the help of an organelle in the cytoplasm called a ribosome, the RNA builds new proteins with the code from the DNA. Each letter of the code is part of a "word" that determines which protein blocks (amino acid) will be used. For example, GGG is a code for glycine. But so is GGC and GGA or GGU. Any of these "words" mean "glycine goes here." It is a system with built-in resilience in that a point mutation of the third letter will not have any effect. There are some RNA codes that are less resilient, with only two possible words coding for the same amino acid.

Though there are many hundreds of possible amino acids, only 22 of them are genetically coded. These can be assembled in various configurations to become proteins ranging in size from about 30 amino acids (usually referred to as peptides) to 30,000 amino acids. They are incredibly diverse and their function is determined almost entirely by their shape. Proteins can be enzymes that regulate chemical reactions. They can be signals, such as insulin that sends signals to other cells from the cell in which it was created. Antibodies are proteins that work with the immune system. Cartilage is made of protein and serves a variety of functions in the skeleton, and keratin, also a protein, is the material of hair and nails.

Because DNA codes for RNA that codes for protein, a mutation in the DNA can cause an error in the protein. Most of the time, the mutation

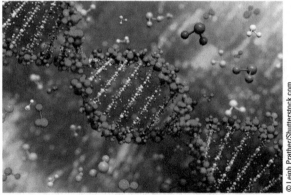

Book analogy: "Nucleotides of DNA are like the letters of the alphabet. Protein molecules are the sentences they spell. Combinations of proteins are the paragraphs. The structures and processes that are organized into different systems with specific tasks (such as digestion or transport) are the chapters of the book, and the complete book is the organism. Natural Selection is the author and editor of all the books in the library of life" (Life, the science of biology 8th ed).

is harmful in some way. Sometimes it has no effect whatsoever. And only sometimes, not very often, a mutation can benefit the owner of that DNA in some way. The environment needs to be just right for whatever that mutation causes. A "good" mutation can be "bad" if the environment is not right. Imagine, for example, a mutation that makes a brown bear have white fur but that bear lives in a boreal forest; potentially beneficial mutation, wrong environment.

Good mutations, though rare, have been piling up for over 3 billion years to give us the diversity that we see around us. It is because of this mind-boggling amount of time that has passed and the unimaginable number of occasions that organisms have reproduced that such a rare event can have such a significant outcome.

And that is how it happens. Simple really. Over time, mutations keep on happening. The bad ones (called deleterious) get weeded out pretty quickly from a population. This is because a bad mutation that decreases an individual's ability to reproduce will likely either not reproduce at all (a really bad mutation) or will produce fewer offspring than those individuals that do not have the bad mutation. Over time, this mutation will be eliminated. Conversely, beneficial mutations will result in more offspring carriers and it will proliferate within the population. Neutral mutations will have no bearing on reproduction and therefore will either increase, decrease, or remain constant by random chance.

Proteins and the Central Dogma

Proteins perform a wide range of functions within living organisms. Among many other vital tasks, they replicate DNA, have structural roles, and are messengers to neighbouring cells and transport molecules. Proteins are made up of one or more peptides, which are further made up of amino acids. Some amino acids are made by the organism while others are obtained through diet.

The process of making proteins from peptides, encoded in DNA is known as the Central Dogma. The Central Dogma consists of two sequential processes: transcription and translation. Transcription is responsible for making

messenger ribonucleic acid, or mRNA, from a gene template. Remember that a gene is a segment of the DNA that codes for a peptide.

The entire process of transcription occurs within the nucleus of the cell, which is, if you remember, where DNA is found. During transcription several

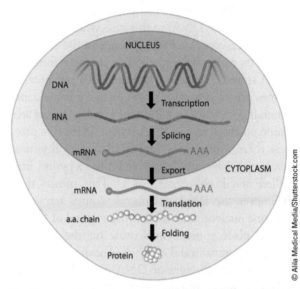

The blueprint that codes for protein is found in the nucleus of the cell and is called DNA. The DNA is transcribed to make RNA, which brings a print out of the protein recipe outside the nucleus for assembly. It is in the cytoplasm of the cell that the RNA is translated and the protein is built.

Use this wheel to "build a protein."

complexes called transcription factors attach onto the DNA near what is called the "TATA box," or a grouping of thymine and adenine nucleotide bases. Theses transcription factors enable RNA polymerase to bind to the DNA, which temporarily unwinds the DNA and replicates a single strand to create a single-stranded mRNA. mRNA is made of nucleotides that are complimentary to the nucleotides of the DNA. In this case, whenever RNA polymerase comes across a guanine in the DNA, it places its reciprocal, cytosine, on the new-forming RNA strand. Similarly, when the RNA polymerase comes across a cytosine it will place a guanine, and when it comes across a thymine it will place an adenine on the forming RNA strand. With this process there is one exception. RNA has no thymine nucleotide base, and in its stead it has a pyrimidine called uracil, abbreviated as U. This means that whenever the RNA polymerase comes across an adenine nucleotide in the template strand of DNA, it will place a uracil nucleotide on the forming complimentary strand of RNA. Another difference between the structure of DNA and RNA is that RNA is single stranded with nucleotides sticking off of it, like a ladder cut in half or one side of a zipper. The result of transcription is a half ladder or open zipper-like strand of mRNA, which will then leave the nucleus via pores in the nuclear envelope and begin the translation.

Once mRNA is in the cytoplasm of the cell, ribosomes attach to the mRNA and translation begins. The ribosome reads the mRNA in groupings of sections of three nucleotides, called codons. Each triplicate of nucleotides, or codon, refers to a specific amino acid to add or a task for the ribosome to complete. The codons tell the ribosome when to start building the peptide with the "Start Codon," which amino acids come next based on specific nucleotides in the codon, and when the peptide is finished, with a "Stop Codon." Once the amino acid chain, or peptide, is formed it will be intricately folded, and either connected to other peptides to form a larger protein, or become a protein on its own. Further down the road, or once the protein tasks have been completed, the protein can be broken down by other proteins and the amino acids will be recycled in order to make future proteins.

Mutation

Hermann J. Muller was an American geneticist who worked on the effects of radiation on physiology and genetics of organisms. In 1926, Muller started radioactively inducing mutations in the DNA of fruit flies to study the physical make-up of genes. He mated the mutated fruit flies with non-irradiated flies to observe the effects of those mutations in offspring. He successfully induced more than 100 mutations. But how do these mutations occur? Muller proposed that the radiation interrupted how the gene works by altering the gene structure or degrading the gene entirely. For this work, Muller was awarded a Nobel Prize.

What is a mutation? A **mutation** is an error in the DNA code. It is a change in the genetic material, which can occur in many different ways. The first type of mutation that can occur is a **point mutation.** Point mutations change only a single letter in the DNA sequence. As we previously learned, DNA is built of four possible letters A, T, G, and C. A point mutation is a change in one of these letters. The effect of these types of mutations depends on where they occur in the strand of DNA. The change in one base pair alters only one part of the amino acid code **(codon),** therefore potentially altering only one amino acid, but not necessarily.

Frameshift mutations are far more detrimental than point mutations. As we learned previously, DNA is read in triplet codons. If a frameshift mutation occurs, meaning that there is

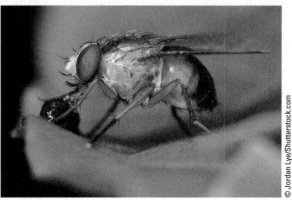

Fruit fly.

Assignment 3: Building protein.

Name: _____   Student Number: _____

Work through the following steps of transcription and translation to find out which proteins are coded for in the DNA strand. Use the amino acid wheel.

If you are given the following DNA strand, can you figure out what the complementary strand would be?

C	C	C	A	C	G	T	A	G	C	C	C	A	A	A	G	G	G	T	T	T	C	G	A	T	G	G	G	T	T

Can you follow this through to build the RNA that would result from the reading of the complementary DNA strand?

If the above is your RNA, which amino acids will you end up with (use the wheel)?

_____

_____

_____

Congratulations! You have now decoded a tiny fragment of a protein blueprint.

What is a protein?

_____

_____

List three proteins and their respective function

_____

_____

Marking:

1) Is the RNA sequence correct?

2) Is the amino acid sequence correct?

3) Accurate and complete definition of a protein

4) Accurate examples of three proteins and their functions

a base pair deleted or inserted into the sequence, then the triple codon read is changed and the gene will be misread. This causes a change in the amino acid sequence, and possibly the function of the protein being created.

Let us take a break from all this molecular stuff and think about the "big picture." We will tie it all together a bit later. The appropriate segue for this shift is to ask "*so what?*" Does it really matter what letter is where in a strand of DNA? Does it really matter if, on occasion, there is an error in copying the code? Let us set these questions aside for a moment and think about the differences among species and how all of that might have come about.

Lamarck and His Giraffes

Darwin is well known for his contribution to evolutionary thinking with the controversial "On the Origin of Species," but before there was Darwin, others were toying with the idea that **Creationism** did not explain life as it was. In 1801, a French scientist by the name of Jean Baptiste Lamarck was one of the first to take a stab at evolutionary theory.

In fact, he was one of the first to use the word "biology" with reference to the concepts now understood to be included in the term. A scholar of plant and invertebrate biology, it is not at all surprising that Lamarck noticed similarities and important differences among species. He was the first to put forward a plausible hypothesis regarding the way in which organisms change over time. It has been shown that his mechanism is incorrect, though recent discoveries in the field of epigenetics provide a delightful opportunity to debate whether some of his ideas are found in natural systems. Lamarck's mechanism for evolution was called "use or disuse."

Picture this. Giraffes. Roaming. Roaming the land in search of luscious foliage. The herd discovers a cluster of tall trees with branches high up above their heads. They are unable to reach them from a relaxed standing position.

So the giraffes have to stretch their necks to reach the plants to survive. Lamarck believed that over time, because of constant use, the stretching of the giraffe's neck would be passed on to the next generation, and with each new generation the neck of the giraffe would get longer and longer. This is the "use" portion of his theory.

The "disuse" is the exact opposite. Lamarck thought that an organ no longer needed would shrink—this is the concept of **vestigial** structures.

A statue of Jean Baptiste Lamarck in the Jardin des Plantes, Paris.

The neck of the giraffe was used by Lamarck as an example of "use or disuse."

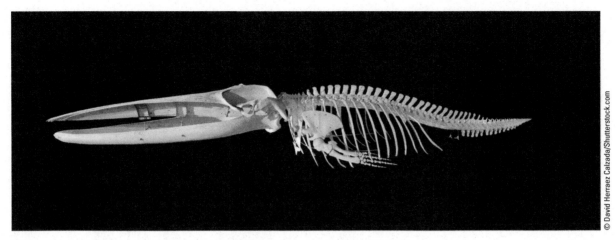

Whales have vestigial organs: at the base of the tail you can see remnants of hind legs.

Can you think of any examples of use or disuse? Several animals have vestigial organs, and humans are not excluded. Toothed whales, such as the sperm whale and baleen whales, like the humpback still have hind legs in their skeletons and all the bones of fingers in their pectoral fins.

Flightless birds, up to 40 different species, still have wings and include penguins, cassowaries, and ostriches. In the absence of predators on isolated land masses such as islands (or Antarctica), these birds no longer needed to fly. With the exception of burrowing, flight is the most costly method of transportation. It represents an impressive energy drain. Therefore, there would be an advantage to "losing" that way of getting around if it were not necessary. So penguins and other flightless birds did not need their wings and this was used by Lamarck to support his "disuse" part of the theory.

How can humans be included in Lamarck's "use or disuse" theory? Humans have teeth we no longer need (wisdom teeth), vestigial tail bones

The wings of penguins, ostriches, and cassowaries are no longer used for flight. Instead, they are used for swimming or sexual display.

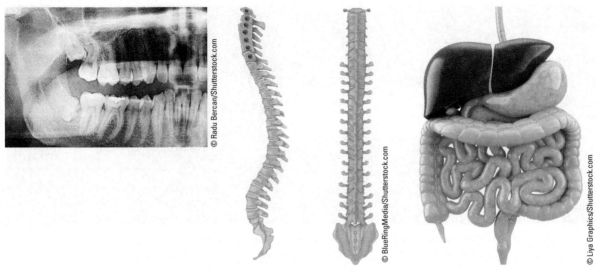

Humans possess a few vestigial organs, remnants of structures that once served important functions. Wisdom teeth (left: impacted), tail bone (center), appendix (small protrusion on bottom left of image; right).

with no tails (coccyx), and the appendix which is thought to have evolved for the breakdown of cellulose and related plant material, is an organ we can happily survive without.

Lamarck also proposed that life evolved over time from simple to complex (i.e. microbes evolved into humans). This was a novel idea in a time when people believed that the universe was the result of divine creation with both simple and complex organisms having been created at the same time.

But does evolution proceed towards increasing complexity? In some cases yes, but in some cases no. The idea that evolution directs a species towards higher complexity is false; there is no direction. It may be just by chance that an organism has evolved into a more complex version. If a more complex structure is beneficial in a certain environment, then it is possible that those individuals possessing slight increases in complexity would be more successful. For example, if the species would be better adapted to an environment by developing more complex organs (i.e. the vertebrate eye), then the changes that occur would likely favour complexity. For other organisms, a simpler environment may call for a more simplistic body plan and a less complex change. The species no longer requires the trait in order to be successful in their environment, so the structure

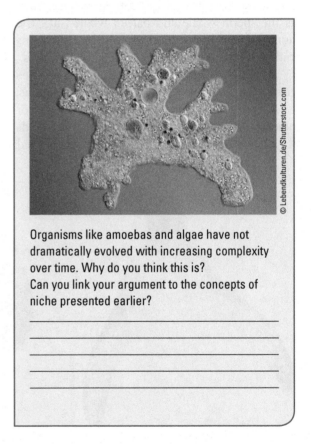

Organisms like amoebas and algae have not dramatically evolved with increasing complexity over time. Why do you think this is?
Can you link your argument to the concepts of niche presented earlier?

_____
_____
_____
_____
_____

regresses, over generations of individuals who are selected for their slightly regressed structure especially if it is costly.

Although his theories now lack acceptance, especially with the emergence of genetic mechanism of **inheritance**, Lamarck opened up the conversation about the changeability of species that eventually led to the theory of **evolution**. He was one of the first people to argue that animals needed to change or alter their behaviour to survive with environmental change, and was one of the first people to suggest that **traits** were **heritable** and passed on from **parent** to **offspring**. This is one of the fundamental tenants of evolution, later developed by Darwin.

Darwin and His Finches

In the early 1800s, there was very little distinction made between scientific and religious thought as it is in many parts of the world today. During the time when Darwin was alive, it was "known" that we were created and placed upon this earth by a higher power. Alternative explanations were mostly unexplored. Every species was believed to have been perfectly designed for its particular environment. It was a common thought within the sciences that the world was static in its current state, not dynamic and changing, as we know it to be today. But slowly, the notion that the world was unchanging was challenged by an accumulation of evidence suggesting otherwise.

Sir Charles Darwin was considered a lazy and slow learner as a child, though he had an interest in natural history and geology. In fact, Darwin was pulled out of school at the age of 16 for being an entirely unremarkable student. He achieved poor grades, rarely participated, and did not pay attention in class. Regardless, Darwin possessed a keen and observant mind whose future observations revolutionized science and created the field of evolution. Following a family tradition, Darwin attended university to study medicine, but he dropped out. Without any other plans Darwin's family persuaded him to become a clergyman and he was excited about this prospect, because he would be able to study natural history while maintaining a socially elevated status. Much to his family's chagrin, at age 22 and before

Charles Darwin (1809–1882)

becoming a member of the clergy, Darwin got a job as a naturalist on the HMS Beagle, a ship that was mapping the coast of South America from 1831 to 1835. What an adventure! Imagine packing up for a long journey around the world with you as the ship's naturalist. Your job? It is to collect and study the wildlife that you encounter on your long walks on shore as you explore new beaches and isolated islands.

While working on the HMS Beagle, Darwin noted many things that challenged the belief that the world and its species were unchanging and perfectly designed for the environment in which they lived. In conflict with the idea that a god had created species perfectly adapted to particular environments, Darwin observed that species in South America were similar to those he saw in England, despite their vastly different habitats. In Maldonado, Uruguay, Darwin came across a fossil of an extinct species, the giant ground sloth. He was baffled. He wondered why the giant ground sloths did not exist anymore. It was obvious that food was not a limiting factor. Did the environment change? What caused those changes? How did these animals die off? The fact that any animal could become extinct conflicted with the idea that a god had made every animal in a perfect state, especially with the added belief that the environment was static.

Puzzled by the distribution of wildlife and fossils, and convinced that there must be some kind of process at play, Darwin began to develop the idea of natural selection. Natural Selection

> **Did you know . . .**
>
> Captain FitzRoy, Captain of the HMS Beagle, nearly rejected Darwin's application to fill the naturalist position on the HMS Beagle after meeting Darwin. His reason? The shape of Darwin's nose! He doubted "anyone with a nose such as Darwin's could possess sufficient energy and determination for the voyage."

can be defined as a process through which organisms better adapted to survive produce more offspring. Natural Selection is a mechanism of evolution and it is not the only way that species can change. We will discuss some of them shortly. One shortfall of Natural Selection is that it cannot anticipate what character traits will be best for future generations; the variation among individuals upon which it acts is totally random. What may be advantageous for one cohort or generation may not be beneficial for the next. Additionally, at the time that Darwin conceived of his theory of Natural Selection, the method by which

The giant ground sloth, now extinct, is evidence of a dynamic environment.

© AuntSpray/Shutterstock.com

Assignment 4: Fill in the map.

Name: _____   Student Number: _____

Do a bit of research to determine the itinerary of the HMS Beagle. Draw the path on the map. Label the important ports of call and the dates.

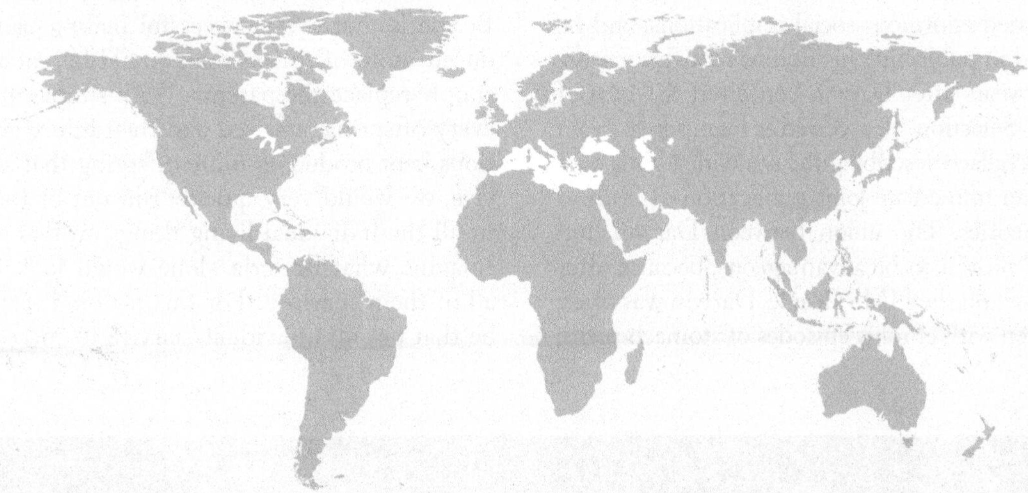

© RAEVSKY/Shutterstock.com

Having done the research on the voyage, what is one thing that you learned about Charles Darwin that was relevant to his discovery?

_____

_____

_____

What is one thing that you learned about Darwin's observations that led to his discovery?

_____

_____

_____

Marking:

1) Is the route correct?

2) Was something (of importance) learned?

genetic information was stored or passed on to offspring was unknown. We now know that traits are passed on through genes, which are encoded in chromosomes within each cell. The physical appearance of a character or a trait is called the phenotype of an individual. The genetic encoding for the phenotype is stored in the DNA of organisms and is called the genotype.

Darwin knew that his theory of Natural Selection carried enormous social implications, and he hesitated in publishing his findings for this reason. Twenty years after Darwin conceived the idea of Natural Selection he received a manuscript from Alfred Wallace describing the same idea. This motivated an immediate joint publication of both of their theories. The union between Darwin and Wallace proved to be advantageous, because after the voyage on the HMS Beagle, Darwin was often bedridden with chronic episodes of stomach pains,

vomiting, severe boils, and other serious health issues. Due to Darwin's unpredictable health, Alfred Wallace was charged with lecturing about and defending their theories to the academic world.

Natural, Sexual, and Artificial Selection

One observation that Darwin made on the HMS Beagle is that every successful mating pair produced more offspring than would be enough to simply replace the parents. With simple math, if every offspring survived and then future generations kept producing more offspring that all survive, we would very quickly run out of room to fit all the individual living things on this planet. Imagine what bacteria alone would look like if all of them survived! For this reason, it can only be that not all individuals survive to successfully

© David Evison/Shutterstock.com

Turtles produce far more eggs than are needed to simply replace the parents, yet the population tends to remain stable if not influenced by human activity.

Assignment 5: Think about it...

Name: _____   Student Number: _____

How was Mendel's work relevant to the theory of Natural Selection?

_____
_____
_____
_____
_____
_____
_____
_____
_____
_____
_____
_____
_____
_____
_____
_____
_____
_____
_____
_____
_____
_____
_____
_____

Marking:

1) Is there a logical connection between Mendel's work and the theory of natural selection?

contribute to the next generation. What could determine which individuals contribute to the next generation? Putting luck aside, some individuals must be more suited, or a better fit for their environment. This idea is coined by the popular phrase "survival of the fittest," meaning that those individuals most fit for their environment will leave more offspring behind with their set of traits. So it follows that in order for some individuals to be better suited to survive than others, there must be variation among individuals within a population. Additionally, if the proportion of traits is going to change over many generations, then these traits must be able to be passed from the parents to the offspring.

Evolution through Natural Selection means that the individual organisms in a population that are best suited for their environment pass on their traits to successive generations. Individuals that are less adapted to their environment will be less successful in passing their traits on to the next generation. It is important to note that very rarely do those less adapted fail entirely to reproduce. Therefore, we deal largely with proportions rather than presence or absence of traits. Over time, the more favourable traits will increase in the population because they tend to have more offspring. In many cases,

therefore, Natural Selection can ultimately reduce the amount of genetic variation present in a population in favour of that variant that favours survival.

For Natural Selection to occur, there must be four conditions. Without one of them, Natural Selection will not occur but evolution might very well. It is important to note that the four conditions fold into each other and overlap.

(1) Overproduction of offspring: individuals must make more offspring than are required to sustain the population. For example, horseshoe crabs produce up to 120,000 eggs, definitely more than needed. If all of them survived, we would be overrun by horseshoe crabs. This, however, is not the case. There must be some kind of reduction of the number of horseshoe crabs in order to keep the population in check.

(2) Variation in the population: individuals within the population must possess variation in their traits. For example, some horseshoe crabs might be more camouflaged than others due to slight differences in colouring, or pattern.

(3) Heritability of variation: it follows that the variation needed in the population must be heritable from the previous generation This means that the offspring of any parent combination must be able to inherit the differences that

© Ilya D. Gridnev/Shutterstock.com

Horseshoe crab.

The number of eggs that a bird lays represents a compromise between increasing reproductive success immediately or in the future.

Having tusks was once an advantage to survival on the African savannah. Nowadays it can get you killed. This tuskless elephant is not in danger of becoming part of the elephant poaching trade and will pass on her lack of tusks to her offspring.

make up the parents. So, for example, horseshoe crabs that are lighter than the others in the population, must be able to pass along this light colouration to their offspring in order for it to be considered heritable.

(4) Differential survival: this variation must result in differential survival. If, for example, horseshoe crabs were indeed of different colours (variation) that were determined by the colours of their parents (heritability) but it made no difference to whether they were eaten by predators or not (no differential survival), then you would not see evolution as a result of Natural Selection. If, however, colour was very important in providing protection from predators, then over time you would expect the population to have more individuals with that adaptive colouring.

The end result of this recipe is the increase in adaptive traits that favour survival in the environment in which they evolved. Change the environment? This results in a new set of survival rules that may or may not lead to further changes.

There are three ways Natural Selection can direct a trait, all based on the effect of *selection* on the characteristics within the population. In *stabilizing selection,* the *medial* trait, or the average trait, is the most successful. Making eggs can be rather "expensive" from an energy perspective. It takes significant body reserves to produce them, keep them warm, and protect them. If a bird, for example, lays too few eggs, then she might not have any of them survive to propagate the next generation. If, however, she produces too many, then she may compromise her own health and risk not being able to breed again in future years. The best strategy is to produce a number of eggs that represents a compromise.

In *directional selection*, one extreme of a trait is more successful than either the norm or other extreme of the trait and therefore there is an

© Joe Farah/Shutterstock.com

Competition for food resources can lead to disruptive selection in the spadefoot toad.

Assignment 6: Illustrating selection.

Name: _____   Student Number: _____

How could you illustrate the difference between stabilizing, disruptive, and directional selection? One way is to graph the frequency of each of the traits. Can you demonstrate the differences? We will get you started. The first graph represents the variation in a population. Change the curves on the graph to demonstrate what would happen during stabilizing, disruptive, and directional selection. Let us imagine that the trait is tail length of a dog. In the original population, most dogs have medium-length tails, while some have short tails and others have long tails. The curve would look like this:

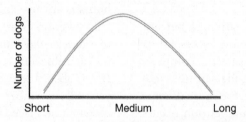

In one sentence, describe what this graph is conveying: _____
_____

Now draw what the effect of stabilizing, disruptive, and directional selection would have on this curve.

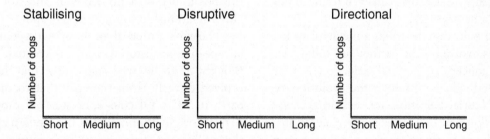

Give one example of a trait that is experiencing: a) stabilising selection, b) disruptive selection, c) directional selection.

_____

_____

_____

Marking:

1) Is the description of the graph correct

2) Are the three graphs correctly drawn?

increase in the frequency of that trait within the population. An example that is happening due to modern human pressures is that of tusklessness in African Elephants. Poaching of elephants for ivory has decreased the reproductive success of tusked elephants while increasing the success of tuskless elephants. Tuskless elephants used to be naturally present within the population at about 1%. Now, in some populations that have been greatly impacted by poaching, they represent up to 40% of individuals. Whereas having tusks used to be rather helpful, nowadays it presents a great risk.

In *disruptive selection*, both extremes, but not the norm of the trait, are the most successful. It seems likely that the more intraspecific competition (competition among individuals of the same species) there is in a population, the more disruptive selection there may be. Competition occurs when there is a limiting resource. This has been found in the spadefoot toads. In ponds that have a high density of the tadpoles, with limited food availability, some tadpoles are exclusively carnivorous while others are herbivorous; the number of omnivores decreases over time. Over many generations disruptive selection can even result in the creation of a new species!

Natural Selection describes a mechanism for how species evolved to be as they are today. An important concept of Natural Selection is that it acts on individuals, although the evolutionary effects of Natural Selection are seen in the entire population and only after many generations. Natural Selection cannot create a novel trait over a single generation, although it can alter the proportion of traits within a population.

If you can visualize far enough back in time, you would find there is a common ancestor among all living animals. That is to say, it is unlikely that life evolved more than once. Of course, during Darwin's time this type of thinking was very much against the social norm and his revolutionary ideas resulted in a great social outcry. In his book *On the Origin of Species*, Darwin suggested that Earth is hundreds of thousands, if not millions of years old! Not only that, but that a god did not make every species perfectly tailored to their environment. Merely surviving to pass on your genes could result in new species? Blasphemy! Most important of all was Darwin saying that we humans are just descendants of the common ape? The nerve of him! Darwin's words had placed humans equal to all the animals of the world. The backlash was fierce and Darwin's name was associated with all sorts of insults, though he did have a few enthusiastic supporters.

After the initial shock, Darwin's theory has become known as a tidy explanation of how species have come to be. And it follows that because humans are also animals, Natural Selection infers a connection from the earlier lines of hominids to modern-day humans. At the time there was no plausible lineage of apes leading to humans. It was absurd to even suggest it! (Even though, if you will remember, Linnaeus suggested a similarity when he placed humans within the group *Anthropomorpha* along with monkeys and apes.) But it was likely because there had not yet been found any "intermediate" species to allow scientists at the time to consider the possibility. Though we are not actually descended from Neanderthal, the discovery of the fossils caused many to consider the possibility of a non-human ancestor and a closer relationship to modern-day apes.

Darwin's proposal of human descent from an ape-like ancestor was misinterpreted. It was thought that he was suggesting that humans evolved directly from the apes that roamed the earth in 1859. Of course, he was not proposing that the origin of human was the modern ape, but that millions of years ago we likely diverged from the same species, with one line evolving to what are now apes and the other to what are now humans. Many members of society floundered for a rebuttal, and one that arose in response to Darwin's ideas is actually pretty good: There are traits that exist in species that are quite maladaptive to survival. In fact, many traits actually impede the survival of the individual. The tail feathers of the male African paradise fly-catcher make it very difficult for the bird to fly, and therefore hard for him to escape predators, whereas the female does not have such elaborate tail feathers. How could this trait not only arise but also spread while decreasing survivorship? Darwin's Natural Selection and the survival of the fittest had to be wrong if something as "unfit" as a long tail could exist. This observation was used to try to refute Darwin's proposed mechanism and, for a time, there was no rebuttal. Thinking about the peacock's tail, according to some accounts, made Darwin "sick to his stomach".

But Darwin figured it out. In his book *The descent of man and selection in relation to* sex,

Darwin presents his ideas on how an organism could have a trait that at first glance seems so unfit for its personal survival. **Sexual Selection** is considered an extension of Natural Selection as it affects the reproductive success of some individuals over others based on their traits or abilities. This time, instead of the environmental conditions determining who survives to reproduce, the decision is made based around mate choice. There are two ways in which to figure out who gets to

The male (top) paradise fly catcher has a long tail used to attract females (bottom). It increases his chances of being predated. But this is the "point" of his "message."

breed with whom. The first way is by intersexual selection: where one member of the mating pair chooses a mate based upon the assessment of their fitness. In the case of the African paradise fly catcher, the females are attracted to the males with the longest tail and choose to breed with the individual with the longest tail that is available to them. Over time, it follows that the males of the species will have longer tails. This is not to say that those males with relatively short tails will die off. It is to say that those males with relatively short tails do not pass on their genes for short tails nearly as frequently as those with long tails. So the proportion of long-tailed males will increase as the proportion of short-tailed males will decrease. A tail, you see, represents a strong message. It says "I am strong, fast, and healthy, despite having this ridiculously long tail. Mate with me and your offspring will be just as fit."

The second way is by intrasexual selection: The decision about who gets to mate with whom is made by competition. The competitors battle it out for the rights to mate with the receptive individuals in the area. Male elephant seals battle amongst each other in dramatic and often quite violent exchanges. The strongest male earns the right to breed with the female seals and a battle with another male can really pay off; male elephant seals can have harems of up to 100 females!

Though Darwin witnessed these scenarios in the wild, much of his inspiration came from considering the changeability of domesticated

Due to artificial selection, pigeons come in all shapes and sizes.

Domesticated dogs come in all shapes and sizes; all of which have been selected artificially.

species. Within domestic species, there is quite a lot of variation of traits. In fact, in order to be able to create different varieties, the more the natural variation, the better. Darwin considered, specifically, the domestic pigeon. Pigeon breeding, at the time, was regarded as a gentleman's activity of the upper class, and in addition to making observations of the breeding programs of these hobbyists, Darwin bred pigeons and kept careful records of his work. Darwin focused on the "selective breeding" mechanism that can lead to domestication. With selective breeding, the breeder identifies and breeds only those individuals that bear the desired traits (e.g. feathers on the feet). The traits themselves are not "created" by the breeder but, rather, once they appear by random mutation, they are "managed" such that the descendants of those bred express the desired trait in greater proportion.

For instance, fur length and colouring are highly variable among breeds of dogs but fairly consistent within the breed. Beginning perhaps as far back as 30,000 years ago, maybe even longer (the date has been shifting around as new evidence is found), humans have been selectively breeding dogs based on their characteristics to get a desired outcome. The puppies that expressed the desired characteristic were then bred with other dogs that also had it until a breed standard was created. This intervention, where people decide which individuals will breed, is called Artificial Selection. Unlike Natural Selection or Sexual Selection, the reproductive success of individuals depends on human choice rather than the ability to physically survive or successfully find a mate. Humans have been selectively breeding animals for centuries. If you look at nearly any domestic species, it is the result of generations of deliberate breeding to foster a particular trait.

Evolution by Other Means

Evolution is the change in gene frequencies in populations. Natural Selection is one way in

which this can be achieved. One thing that the forms of selection that we discussed have in common is that they are non-random processes. That is, there is "selection" involved. The next processes that we are going to describe are much more, if not entirely, random.

Gene flow

Gene flow is the exchange of genes between populations and between species. Migration of organisms into and out of populations can cause a change in the proportion of traits within that population. Organisms that have greater mobility have increased gene flow than populations whose individuals are restricted in some way.

Gene flow can be restricted by geographic barriers including mountains, oceans, and deserts or anthropogenic (human made) including structures like fences or highways. Gene flow can also be restricted by speciation and the inability to hybridize or produce viable offspring in a hybrid situation. For example, a zonkey is a cross between a donkey and a zebra. The offspring cannot successfully reproduce; therefore, gene flow is limited after the first generation.

Sexual selection can also limit gene flow. Females often chose males based on their physical attributes, thus propagating certain genes throughout the population.

Zonkey: a hybrid between a zebra and a donkey.

Genetic drift

Genetic drift is the change in the frequency of traits in a population because of random sampling. What this means is that when parents produce offspring with a sample of the parental traits, there is potentially a random chance of the offspring survival. Genetic drift may cause a trait to disappear completely, thus reducing genetic variation. As opposed to Natural Selection, genetic drift is thought to play a minor role in evolution due to its random nature.

One way to understand genetic drift is to picture marbles in a jar. In the jar, there are 40 marbles, 20 red and 20 blue. The colours represent different traits. After each generation the organisms reproduce randomly. To populate the second jar, you randomly select colours of marbles to represent the offspring. You can see with each generation that the red colour becomes less and less frequent in the jars. This is genetic drift: changes in trait frequency due to random events.

There are important types of genetic drift: bottlenecks and founder effect. Remember that both of these are random.

A population **bottleneck** is caused by a drastic reduction in population size due to an environmental catastrophe such as earthquakes, floods, or droughts. This mass reduction in the population causes a loss of genetic variation in a population due to random removal. A smaller population remains with lower genetic variation, passing on a reduced genetic diversity to offspring. This lack of genetic diversity can leave this small population vulnerable to future environmental changes.

During the 18th and 19th centuries, most of the world's populations of fur seals were

Fur seals were nearly hunted to extinction in the 17th and 18th centuries. Though many of these species have since recovered their numbers, their genetic variation has been dramatically reduced.

hunted to near extinction. In that time, the fur from the fur seal was used to make felt. Felt hats had become popular in Europe, and to keep the population's heads warm, furs from a variety of species were used. Like the rest of the fur seal species, the Guadalupe fur seal population suffered from the hunt: 52,000 individuals were hunted until the mid-1800s. Presumed extinct, some were surprised to discover a small breeding population in 1928 that was then destroyed with takes by zoos and museums. Thought again to be extinct, a tiny population of 14 seals was discovered in 1954 and from that has sprung a population of now over 12,000 individuals. But how "healthy" is this population? How genetically resilient could it be?

The **founder effect** is another form of diminished genetic variation. It involves a new population being formed by only a few individuals that change their location from the original population. Given enough time, this could lead to a speciation event, where this smaller population evolves into a species that is no longer reproductively compatible with the original population.

Founder effects can be seen in islands where small subsets of larger populations settle with little to no input of new genetic diversity. Founder effects can be detected in the world's human population. The African gene pool contains the greatest variation. It is thought that those individuals

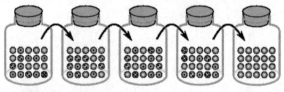

Genetic drift: the random sampling of a population's variation that is not representative of the original proportions.

Assignment 7: What is the difference?

Name: _____   Student Number: _____

Try drawing it out: below are two "initial populations." Population A will experience a bottleneck and population B will undergo a founder effect. Alter the illustration to demonstrate this concept.

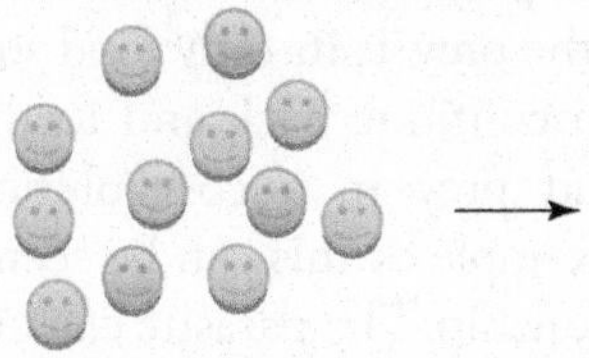

A    **B**

In both initial populations, what is the ratio of ☺ to ☺? _____

Now take your smiley population through either a bottleneck (Population A) or a founder effect (Population B)

Answer the following:

In Population A, what is the frequency of ☺? _____
In Population B, what is the frequency of ☺? _____

In Population A, what is the frequency of ☺? _____
In Population B, what is the frequency of ☺? _____

In Population A, what is the ratio of ☺ to ☺? _____

In Population B, what is the ratio of ☺ to ☺? _____

In bottleneck effect, how many populations remain? _____
In founder effect, how many populations remain? _____

Based upon the above ratios, out a paragraph to describe the difference between bottleneck and founder effect

_____
_____
_____
_____
_____

Need a bit more help? there is a lot to check online!

Marking:

1) Are the effects properly represented in the populations?
2) Is the explanation of the difference correct and based upon the ratios above?

that migrated out of Africa settled first in what is now called India. Here is the world's second highest amount of genetic variation. And so, this pattern continues until we get to the very southern tip of South America, each migration "bout" containing a smaller sample of the original population with a skewed distribution of variation that is not representative.

Some Interesting Points

There are some interesting questions that arise from common misconceptions when discussing the theory of evolution. For example, if fish became amphibians through the process of evolution and natural selection, then why do fish still exist? Fish still exist because present-day fish and present-day reptiles share a common ancestor. Both lines have been evolving for the same amount of time. Just because some fish evolved to become amphibians and reptiles does not mean all of them did. If, for example, the beach contained an untapped source of food from washed-up organisms, then an animal capable of surviving in air, even for a short time, would have a competitive advantage over animals that could not. Amphibians and fish have evolved to occupy different niches based on their needs and their abilities to successfully survive and thrive.

So similarly, when someone asks, "if we are descended from monkeys, why are there still monkeys?" the answer is the same as above. We are not descended from monkeys, we share a common ancestor with monkeys that lived about 6 mya.

Can evolution of one species affect the evolution of another? YES! This is often called an evolutionary arms race when referring specifically to predator/prey relationships. For example, a prey species may evolve a strategy to harm (i.e. toxins, spines, etc.) the predator that relies upon them for food. In response to this, the predator may also evolve to counter the prey's defense mechanisms if it relies heavily on the prey as its only food source. This arms race can continue back and forth between predator and prey in a co-evolutionary process. Another example of this can be seen in a host–parasite relationship. The parasite can evolve more effective ways of exploiting the host, while the host will co-evolve in response to the parasite and develop better ways of detecting and destroying the parasite. This again will continue going back and forth between host and parasite.

Are species still evolving? Yes! Even though it may seem as though we are a stagnant species, we are continuously changing. It is easier to appreciate the sequence of changes that led to our evolution in the past because we can appreciate the drastic changes, say from early hominids like *Australopithecus* to today's *Homo sapiens*. A lot of our more recent changes have occurred at the molecular level to cope with stressors, for example, lactose intolerance, disease resistance, sickle cell anemia, and malaria.

The Species Problem

Now that we have discussed the concepts of evolution and the theories behind how species evolve, we can look at the natural world and appreciate

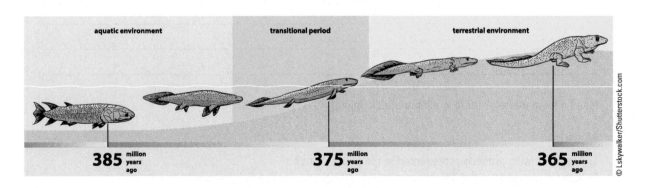

just how many species there are. Estimates range anywhere from 5 to 10 million different species currently living. If we were to count all those that are now extinct, the number is unimaginable. But what is a species? How is one recognized? How do we classify organisms into different species when things can look so similar? Is a domestic cat a different species than a domestic dog? What about a Chihuahua and a Great Dane? Here we will outline a few of the most important species concepts. These have arisen because sometimes the classic biological species concept is less relevant in certain groups of organisms. When reading the following species concepts, it is important to keep in mind how these species concepts can be applied to the real world and the implications of each of them.

Biological Species Concept

The biological species concept defines the term as interbreeding natural populations, which are reproductively isolated from each other. Basically, the individuals in question have to be able to breed successfully with viable (able to reproduce) offspring. This is a testable concept because it is based on mechanism; either the resulting offspring can produce viable offspring or not. So, in this case, domestic dogs are all members of the same species because they produce viable offspring when they interbreed. A donkey and a horse, however,

"I was much struck how entirely vague and arbitrary is the distinction between species and varieties"— Charles Darwin, On the Origin of Species (p. 48)

though offspring are produced (mules), are not of the same species because the mule is sterile. This, at first glance, seems simple enough. But there are nuances and situations that test the usefulness of this definition.

Mules, the product of a cross between a horse and a donkey, cannot produce viable offspring.

Are all of these dogs members of the same species?

Though lions and tigers are able to reproduce, they are considered separate species because their natural ranges do not overlap. In addition, male ligers are often sterile.

The biological species concept becomes tricky when looking at different forms of speciation, which have been discussed previously. The biological species concept can be used to describe species created through sympatric speciation (speciation without geographical barriers) and parapatric species (can interbreed but do not), but cannot be used to distinguish among species from allopatric speciation (speciation by geographic barrier resulting in isolation) because they are not presented with the opportunity to interbreed if they could.

What if you never observe the populations reproducing? How can you be sure they produce viable offspring? And how can you define reproductive isolation? This poses a challenge when using the biological species concept. Even when species are separated and seem to be reproductively isolated, there is the potential of interbreeding. This is called **hybridization**, where different species can reproduce, forming a genetic and visual **intermediate** of the two parental species called a hybrid. Hybridization can be common in nature. For example, many fish species can easily hybridize. A brook trout and a brown trout can hybridize, creating a tiger trout, a sterile hybrid.

If you were a conservation biologist, how would you deal with the issues of different species and the application of the biological species concept? What is the implication of hybridization? In the case where the brook and brown trout hybridize, the offspring are reproductively sterile. Does this pose a threat to the two species? How does this influence management?

When considering using the biological species concept to define a species, one must also take into account the issue of **cryptic** species. Cryptic species are two or more species that cannot be distinguished by examining their morphology (physical characteristics), are genetically different,

The tiger trout (top) is a hybrid of the brook trout (middle) and the brown trout (bottom).

but that are unable to interbreed. Cryptic species can be very common in insects, fish, reptiles, and amphibians. For example, the Amazonian frogs classified as *Eleutherodactylus ockendeni* are virtually indistinguishable from each other morphologically, but in fact genetically can be grouped into three different species.

Phenetic species concept

Phenetic species are a set of organisms that look similar to each other and distinct from other sets of organisms. They are usually called **morphospecies** and are classified by their anatomical characteristics alone. Usually, a large number of features, lengths of digits, size of eyes, colours, and shapes, are measured or assessed, and then a cluster analysis is conducted. Simply put, each cluster would be characterized as a species.

Does this method account for the evolutionary history of the species? How would it handle convergent structures?

Frogs of the Amazonian rain forest are difficult to classify because they are morphologically similar. Recent genetic investigations have revealed at least three separate species. This is a case of where the phenetic definition and the biological species definition would yield different results.

Bats, birds, and bees can fly. Does this make them related?

Does this method account for variation within a species? Because the classification is based upon common structures and characters, species with built-in variation are more likely to be divided than grouped. The greater the number of characters with variation, the greater the number of "false" species. A classic example of this is the case of the blue goose. This goose was thought to be a separate species until the 1980s. It turns out that they are the same species and that individuals tend to choose a mate based upon the pairing of their parents. So, a white individual who had mixed parents will mate with a blue goose, or a blue goose descended from two blue geese will mate with another blue.

What about sexual dimorphism? Morphologically, many males and females in the same species look very different. For example, elephant seals. Males are much larger and have a proboscis (trunk-like structure of the nose), while females are substantially smaller and look more like sea lions.

This sexual dimorphism or differences can also be seen in most bird species, where the male is bright and colourful and the female is dull. By identifying a discreet species using strictly anatomic features, males and females could be classified as different species.

If you classified a series of species based strictly upon morphology you may make some rather big mistakes. But under what conditions would this definition be useful? This species concept is good in a pinch, for example when you only have limited time in which to assess diversity, or

The blue goose (right) was once thought to be a separate species.

you do not have the funds necessary to collect genetic samples. You can easily identify most species based on morphological differences, but a more comprehensive analysis will be needed to confirm species identification. How does this species concept work with the possibility of cryptic species? Do you think this is a good species concept to use? Would you be skeptical of conclusions made using this methodology?

Ecological Species Concept

The ecological species concept suggests that species are a set of organisms adapted to exploit the same resources. Remember back to the chapter on niche and how an organism uses and interacts

Elephant seals are highly sexually dimorphic: the males can be up to 4.5 m long while the females are only up to 2 m long.

with its environment? A **niche** is the *role* of an organism in its **environment**. Organisms are adapted to certain environments and certain ecological niches. This concept suggests that these **adaptations** to specific ecological niches will allow species to be distinguished from each other.

> *Lineage or a closely related set of lineages which occupies an adaptive zone minimally different from that of any other lineage in its range and which evolves separately from all lineages outside its range*
>
> (Van Valen 1976)

This is the first species concept to incorporate the role of the environment and the function of the organism into the definition.

Again, one must consider the possibility of cryptic species when using this species concept. One must also consider the dynamics of ecosystems and **niche partitioning**. Species can overlap in resource use and can switch resources when one is depleted. There is often quite a bit of plasticity built into the niche concept. Ecosystem and community ecology can be very complex and this can lead to issues in explicitly defining a species.

For example, a study done by Donald and Alger (1993) suggests that lake trout and bull trout can overlap in their niches resulting in an increase in competition between the two species. Based on the definition of the ecological species concept, with overlapping niches would you consider the bull and lake trout the same species?

Phylogenetic species concept

Phylogenetic species are those that can be distinguished by the smallest identifiable cluster of individual organisms within which there is a common ancestor shared with the next closely related cluster. This species concept considers the evolutionary and ancestral relationships among

Assignment 8: Different fish, same niche?

Name: _____   Student Number: _____

© shanesabin/Shutterstock.com

If all of these fish occupied the same niche, would they be the same species? Apply the basic principles of niche theory and explain your answer.

_____

_____

_____

_____

_____

_____

_____

Marking:

1) Is the concept of niche understood?

2) Is niche concept applied correctly?

organisms. The phylogenetic species concept describes a group of organisms that are genetically isolated, but does not consider reproductive isolation like the biological species concept. In this definition, taken into account is the genetic past and not the present situation.

Now that we know how to classify a species, you might be asking yourself, well, are not all species related? Yes, in a manner of speaking. When talking about the "relatedness" on an evolutionary scale, it is true that all species at one point in time shared a common ancestral species (i.e. humans shared a common ancestral species with chimpanzees and bonobos approximately 6 mya). Current research in genomics has confirmed that all living organisms are derived from a single species. We will investigate the concept of genes in the next part of this text.

Genetic species concept

The genetic species concept claims that species are defined by the amount of genetic differences that exist between groups. This genetic difference

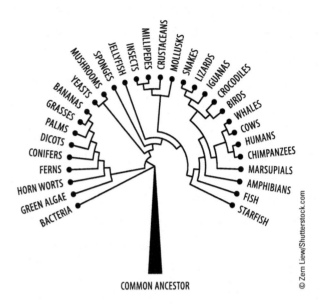

COMMON ANCESTOR

results in reproductive isolation between the two groups, thus distinguishing different species. For two separate groups to be considered two different species, there must be a greater genetic difference between the two groups, then within the two groups.

Moving on to Part II

In the first part of this text we looked at three seemingly unrelated concepts: the ways of knowing, ecology, and evolution.

In Part II, we will tie it all together in telling our story. That is, the story of *Homo sapiens sapiens*. The link between ecology and evolution is key in understanding how we are, what we are, and how we have come to be this way. You see, *evolution happens in the context of ecology.* As we have seen, ecology describes the environment that is experienced by an organism, and it is the biotic and abiotic factors with which it interacts. Evolution, or the changing of a species over time, happens within the environment and because of the environment. They really cannot be separated. And how do we know all of these things? Well, so far, science methodolgy has been pretty useful to help us gain insight.

Throughout the sections, there will be similar themes that emerge. These include that there are actually very few unique qualities (or traits) that define "human." Many of the things that we consider to be uniquely human were not actually "invented" by humans; most of them were, however, perfected by humans. Examples include tool use, fire control, cooking, and perhaps language (a bit of an exception depending upon your definition of "human"). We know that tool use was not invented by humans because evidence of tool use has been found that pre-dates the evolution of *Homo sapiens sapiens*. It may come as no surprise that *Homo habilis* was likely a regular user of tools. But tool use pre-dates even this close relative. We need to go back all the way to a species called *Australopithecus* to start to understand the beginnings of hominid tool use and that is indeed a very long time ago.

Another big theme is that though it may seem as if humans have "stopped" evolving, we continue to change just as we have in the past; it is only the factors selecting the change that are different. This does not only apply to humans of course; many events throughout the millennia have altered the conditions under which species have evolved. The reason for these changing "factors" is a changing environment, or changing ecology. Throughout the history of Earth, the climate has varied dramatically, with long periods of cooling and short periods of warming, fragmentation of the landscape, dropping and rising sea levels, and changes in the composition of the atmosphere. And throughout at least 30% of this time, life has survived. But it has changed as Earth has changed and the factors responsible for those changes have not remained constant over time.

Humans have been changing since we first "arrived" on the scene and we will continue to do so. It is difficult to appreciate the reality of our own evolution because of our relatively short lifespan. We will not be able to witness, for example, the loss of an organ, or the development of a new one. But we can look to history, to archaeology, and anthropology to tell us about how we have changed and what may have been the driving forces behind it. We may be able to make predictions about future changes. But experience has also shown us that we are quite miserable when it comes to accurate predictions on such grand scales. Irrespective, it can be fun to think about it and so we shall.

In this text we will spend more time covering the pre-human species and cover humans during our class time. The reason for this is quite simple: it is simpler to describe the human species in past rather than in modern times. You see, one of the big changes in the human species is that we have become so diverse from an ecological and social perspective. Describing 'humans' of the past takes up less space and therefore keeps this book to a manageable length. But if we were to include all the diversity of humanity that exists today, well, that would require a series of volumes. It is a delightful shame. This text therefore will set the scene for you as we learn about some of the specifics in the evolution of humans and in our relationship with nature.

But first, well, there is a lot of back story to cover. You see, we did not spontaneously pop up on the surface of the Earth to do with it as we will. It took a long, long time. How long depends upon from where you would like to start. And we would like to start from the beginning.

It starts with a BANG!

PART II
Getting to Human—Evolution

The Beginning of the Universe

Oftentimes texts written on the topic of biology begin the story at about 3.8 billion years ago, with excellent reason (because life did not exist before that time). But we are going to go back further because it is an even more exciting place to start. Let us go back approximately 13.8 billion years. This date, as of this very moment that we write, is as far back as any historian has been able to go; this date marks the beginning of the universe. It is not possible to say what existed before the universe or what currently exists beside the universe. Perhaps, like the cycling of our landmasses on Earth through the process of plate tectonics, there were other universes that experienced expansion and then collapse. Take your brain there for a minute: ask yourself *"what was it like before the beginning of this universe?"* Try to imagine a scenario.

Since the time of the great Greek philosophers who examined the night sky and wondered what might account for their observations, many hypotheses have been presented to explain the patterns of movement of stars and planets. Even though the surface of Earth had not yet been mapped, some of their early conclusions were quite accurate including that our galaxy, the Milky Way, is composed of distant stars (Democritus circa 460–370 bce). Aristotle however, believed the Milky Way to be located in the space between the Moon and Earth, an observation that cannot be supported because of the principles associated with *parallaxis*. In fact, it was al-Hassan Ibn al-Haitham, one of the contenders for the distinction of the Father of Science, who determined that the Milky Way did not have a parallax. He concluded that it must therefore be very distant. The concept of parallax played a vital role in the discoveries regarding the nature of the universe when, in 1929,

Since at least 370 BCE, philosophers have been examining our galaxy, the Milky Way, and postulating on its creation and function.

> **Did you know . . .**
>
> Parallaxis refers to the phenomenon of closer objects appearing to move greater distances with the displacement of the observer. More distant objects therefore appear to move shorter distances relative to closer objects. Consider the perceived difference in movement of objects close and far away when you are driving in a car: objects closer to you whizz by, while the distant landscape barely moves.

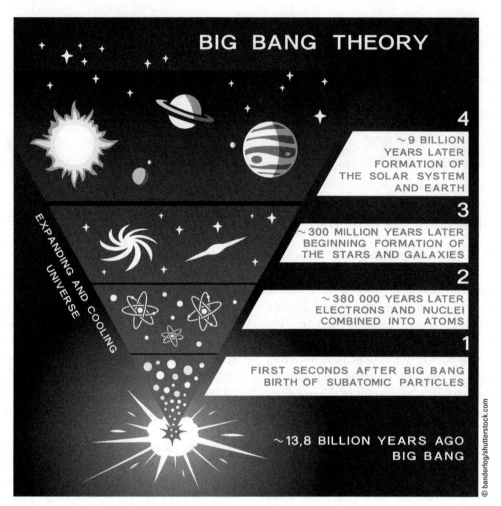

The Big Bang

Edwin Hubble determined that neighbouring galaxies were moving away from our Milky Way. He concluded this by observing that the speed of galaxy dispersal is related to their relative distances from us. Hubble could only account for the movements that he observed by adding in that the universe is expanding. The consequence of this can only be that in the future, neighbouring galaxies will be too distant to observe. But, if we rewind, rather than fast forward, it also implies that at one point in time the universe was tiny. And the only way to reconcile its original "tininess" with its current size (approximately 93 billion light years from end to end) is to postulate that a giant explosion—shall we say a "Big Bang"—is responsible. One of the great questions of modern astrophysics is whether this

expansion will continue indefinitely or whether it will slow down and collapse on itself (a.k.a. the Big Crunch). The problem is that the rate of expansion is actually increasing and this is counter to our understanding of the laws of physics (if mass creates gravity and gravity creates pull, then the movement of expanding mass should slow down).

Irrespective of the uncertainties, scientists are quite certain that a large explosion created the universe that we now know and study and that it is expanding at an increasing rate. When this happened, as matter was travelling outwards, slightly denser areas attracted matter from slightly less dense areas. Over a long period of time masses of matter shaped stars, and bunches of stars made up galaxies. Our solar system formed about 4.5 billion years ago and its formation is attributed to the collapse of a giant, flat, rotating cloud that probably got its "kick start" from a shock wave thrown off by a nearby supernova. The atoms of the rotating cloud sorted themselves out according to their mass with the heaviest atoms remaining closer to the centre and the lighter atoms distributing themselves out towards the margins. Over time, these atoms began to accumulate and as their collective mass increased, gravitational forces increased and planets were formed. Earth, the densest of all the planets, is the only one with confirmed geological activity (plate tectonics), liquid water, and (so far) life.

And here is the key point to answer your question: *why start at the very beginning?*: it is precisely these unique features (geological activity and liquid water) that have allowed life as we have it to evolve. Without the movements of the tectonic plates, a diversity of habitats would not have been available to facilitate the diversification of life, and without liquid water, there would not have been the protection needed from the Sun's harmful radiation. Within the first billion years of Earth's history, biological life was thriving in the oceans. Their collective metabolisms created gases that accumulated in the atmosphere to eventually form the ozone layer. The ozone layer is an essential protector from the Sun's radiation and its formation allowed for life to spread to terrestrial environments.

We are unsure how, exactly, life got started on Earth. Many hypotheses exist, including that RNA precursors arrived on Earth from extraterrestrial sources. But there is one hypothesis that has been investigated scientifically by Dr. Stanley Miller, who at the time (1952), was a 23-year-old graduate student in the Department of Chemistry at the University of Chicago. Before an audience of well-respected (and intimidating) scientists, Miller combined methane, ammonia, hydrogen, and water vapour in a bottle and subjected this mixture to an electric spark. His selection of gases was not random: it simulated what scientists Oparin and Haldane had, in 1920, proposed to represent the composition of a primitive Earth atmosphere. What Miller found in his bottle was truly remarkable: the amino acids glycine and alanine, two building blocks of protein (the most important

component of living tissue). Miller's article was published in the journal *Science* in 1953. This was a remarkable year for evolution science in general: Watson and Crick published their model of DNA and Sanger and his colleagues published the first complete sequence of a protein.

What is clear is that somehow self-replicating molecules evolved into single-celled organisms. And though these single-celled organisms are complex and it is difficult to imagine how they could have assembled, they represent the "simplest" life forms on Earth. They are called *prokaryotes*.

A prokaryote is a very simple organism composed of a single cell. Therefore, it has no organs or organ systems like the animals with which we are familiar. Everything that a prokaryote needs to survive and all of the biological processes including eating, growing, and reproducing are achieved by a single cell. Instead of organs like kidneys and hearts, it has *organelles*. These are tiny structures that have different functions just as organs do within our bodies. In a prokaryotic organism, there is really only one kind of organelle and they float around in the cell's cytoplasm, a liquidy goo that is made up of mostly water. The organelles are called ribosomes and they are responsible for protein production in association with the DNA code. These organelles float in the cytoplasm that is contained by a cell membrane made of lipids (fat). A flagellum is often present to help the organism get around and hunt for food.

Bacteria Cell Anatomy

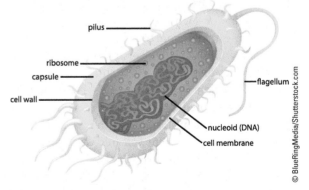

The prokaryotic cell is life's simplest form and is represented by the Bacteria.

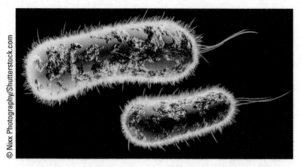

Bacteria were likely the first type of life on Earth and they remain today the most abundant of all lifeforms. Here the flagellum, a kind of "tail," can be easily seen.

Anatomy of an Animal Cell

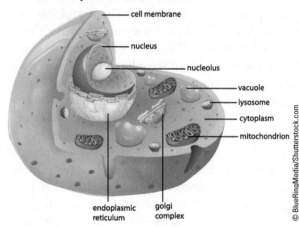

Eukaryotic cells are vastly more complex than the prokaryotic cells.

Though from our perspective bacteria live an invisible life, they are essential to the ecosystem. They occupy a wide variety of niches and it would be impossible to describe them all here. To simplify, bacteria play a vital role in the "recycling" of nutrients and tens of millions of bacteria cells can live in a single gram of soil. It has been estimated that there are between 4 and 6×10^{30} of these cells on the planet, most of which live in the oceans and soil.

Prokaryotes reproduce asexually. They do not combine genetic material from a "father" and a "mother" to produce an offspring. Instead, bacteria usually replicate their own DNA and split the cell into two. This means that differences within the species occur due to mutation, and not the combining of parent DNA. Given the staggering number of bacteria on Earth and the frequency of bacterial asexual reproduction, the potential for the formation of new species is very high.

The oldest fossils found up until right now are those of very early bacteria. The rocks containing the remains of such organisms were found by a team of researchers from the University of Western Australia and Oxford University in a remote area of Western Australia in 2010 and are estimated to be 3.4 billion years old. In life, these bacteria would have formed a purplish mat of slime across the beaches, in an atmosphere with very little oxygen made hot by frequent volcanic eruptions.

It is difficult to fathom that the greatest known difference among organisms on Earth occurs at the level of the cell: Prokaryotes are vastly differentiated from eukaryotes.

Eukaryotes are the cells that make up every species with which we are familiar from the largest whale to the smallest mushroom. The eukaryotes therefore include animals, plants, and fungus but it also includes a large group of single-celled eukaryotic organisms called protists. Let us focus on these for a while. Picture an Amoeba; this is one such organism. It is much more complex than a prokaryote even though it is also just one cell. The differences are that eukaryotic cells have many types of organelles that serve many functions just like the organs of a large animal. The cells are therefore much bigger than prokaryotes. The fragile DNA is kept within the nucleus, a fortress protected by a membrane made of lipids, and other organelles remain suspended in the cytoplasm that is contained also by a cell membrane of lipids. The organelles include mitochondria (responsible for the formation of the organism's primary energy molecule and also contain their own DNA), the golgi complex (responsible for the packaging of proteins before they are sent to their destination), and lysosomes (responsible for the breaking down and processing of waste).

How do we go from prokaryotes to the evolution of eukaryotes? There are some scientists that believe that because these two cell types are so different from each other, they must have had a

Assignment 9: How many bacteria?

Name: _____   Student Number: _____

Think about it . . .

It is estimated that there are between 100,000 and 10,000,000 different species of bacteria.

1) What is a bacterium?

_____

_____

_____

2) What are two benefits of bacteria to humans?

_____

_____

_____

3) Why do you think that there are so many species?

_____

_____

_____

4) Why are we so uncertain about how many species of bacteria there are?

_____

_____

_____

Marking:

1) Accurate and complete description of bacteria
2) Two distinct benefits
3) Plausible reason for why so many species
4) Plausible reason for why we are uncertain

distinct origin. That is, they must have evolved independently. But there is another, quite plausible, explanation that has gained a lot of support. Thought to have occurred 2 billion years after the evolution of the first prokaryotic cells, *endosymbiosis* is, to date, the best theory of how a Eukaryotic cell could have evolved in the context of a prokaryotic ecosystem. Endosymbiosis postulates that several of the organelles of the Eukaryotic cells, including the mitochondria, were actually prokaryotic bacterial organisms that were ingested but not digested inside the soon-to-be-eukaryotic cell. It is a kind of assimilation. The evidence for this theory is indeed quite convincing. The following represents a short version of the list.

Evidence for endosymbiosis

These organelles:

- have their own lipid membranes similar in structure to those of prokaryotes.
- have their own DNA in the form similar to prokaryotes.
- reproduce by asexual reproduction within the cytoplasm.
- if removed from the cytoplasm, cannot be replaced by the cell.

Endosymbiosis therefore represents the first major *Paradigm Shift* in evolution. A paradigm shift actually refers to a major change in scientific thought or a change in perspective that does not allow one to revert back to the original condition. Let us take that principle and apply it to evolution and say that an evolutionary paradigm shift is a major "advancement" such that the niches able to be exploited by such advancement are unlike those previous.

Before endosymbiosis, organisms were very small and rather fragile; prokaryotes are anywhere between 0.00002 and 0.0002 cm long and eukaryotes are an astounding 0.001 – 0.01 cm long. Prokaryotes were not able to reproduce by

sexual recombination of DNA, and though they did exhibit great species diversity, the differences among them were modest. After endosymbiosis and the evolution of eukaryotes, organisms became much larger and therefore more robust, sexual reproduction evolved and a diversity of niches were exploited.

It did not take long (relatively speaking, of course) for the next big paradigm shift in biological evolution: multicellularity. A single-celled organism can only grow so big (though you may be surprised to learn that the largest single-celled organisms, discovered at 10.6 km below the surface of the ocean, measure 10 cm long) and is therefore more vulnerable to the environment (e.g. dehydration), and limited with respect to transportation mechanisms, reproduction, and feeding. Multicellularity is such a successful strategy that it has evolved independently at least 25 times! Fungi, plants, animals, all evolved multicellularity after they split from each other on the evolutionary tree as single-celled organisms. Therefore, identifying the timing of the evolution of multicellularity is complex but it is thought that the eukaryotes were affected approximately 1 billion years ago with a major explosion of diversity occurring 550 million years ago (mya).

There are several possible explanations for how multicellularity could have evolved and, given that it did so independently so many times, it is likely that even more variations exist. Let us focus on coloniality. It is thought that the first aggregation of single cells was actually in the form of a colony of individuals rather than a single organism made up of many cells. Over time, this colony became more permanently fixed together and parts of it began to specialize. With a larger "body," natural selection could act upon different regions of the colony in different ways, selecting individuals for different traits. This selection may have made those individuals unable to survive without their neighbours. Reproduction, for example, could then be limited to a certain region of the colony, digestion to another. This means that those individuals unable to reproduce would rely on the reproductive areas while providing another important services to the colony that was now becoming more and more like a larger, single individual.

A curious organism that might help you to understand what an example of a colonial, though quasi-multicellular organism might resemble is *Volvox*, a microscopic alga found in your local freshwater puddle. Volvox resembles a translucent golf ball with smaller, more opaque golf balls suspended inside. Thought to be composed of single-celled individuals related to a group of organisms called *Chlamydonomas*, it is a colony composed of 1) somatic cells each with a tiny flagellum for locomotion and 2) gonidia, or reproductive cells. The reproductive cells produce daughter colonies, first to the inside of the golf ball where they can be protected from the elements. When it is time to release the daughter colonies, the parent disintegrates and they disperse.

There are definite advantages to a multicellular body. These include:

1) being larger (and therefore able to outcompete smaller organisms and maintain an internal environment protected and perhaps distinct from the external surroundings),
2) cell function differentiation, and
3) increasing complexity.

To achieve multicellularity, however, the evolution of key mechanisms is necessary, including:

1) communication among cells,
2) provisioning of cells with their required nutrients, and
3) controlling the exchange of molecules with the external environment.

These mechanisms are not cheap but they allow for an incredible amount of diversification as is demonstrated by the dramatic increase in multicellular speciation that occurred 550 mya. This diversification is often referred to as the Cambrian Explosion. Up until this time most of the life on Earth was rather small, perhaps colonial or only recently multicellular. During the early years of the Cambrian Period, great innovations (such as armoured plating for protection) evolved. Though recent evidence suggests that we should downplay the "explosiveness" of the increase in diversity, it is nonetheless an important moment in evolutionary history.

Several explanations for the ultimate causes of this explosion have been explored by scientists. Though not a unique event in the history of Earth, a changing atmosphere is attributed to this time period. The atmosphere of Earth did not originally contain oxygen; it was added slowly to the skies by millions of years of photosynthesis beginning with the cyanobacteria and

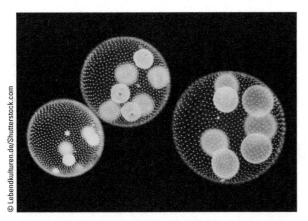

Volvox is a colonial species of up to 50,000 individuals, with differentiated functions.

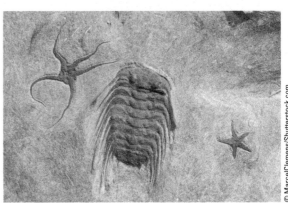

Trilobites are the ambassadors of the Cambrian Explosion.

then the algae, and plants. The concentration of atmospheric oxygen continues to rise because photosynthesis has not stopped. By the time of the Cambrian Explosion it is thought that atmospheric oxygen levels were high enough to 1) facilitate the formation of the ozone layer that blocks harmful radiation from the sun, and 2) allow for the evolution of "hard parts" like the protective shells of trilobites (the oxygen in lower atmospheric concentrations was used for higher priority functions and could not be used for less important systems, such as making shells). Shells and the evolution of external hard parts led to the exoskeleton that is typified by the trilobite: a hard external skeleton to maintain body size and protect from both the elements and predators. It is thought that the evolution of these exoskeletons was advantageous enough to develop under conditions when oxygen was at less of a premium.

A study conducted in 2013 by researchers at the University of Southern Denmark, however, have demonstrated that Earth's atmosphere contained plenty of oxygen as early as 2.1 billion years ago. If true, this would indeed put a bit of a damper on our atmospheric oxygen hypothesis for the cause of the Cambrian Explosion. But does it really?

Another explanation originates with evidence of rising sea levels and, therefore, a reduction in competition for space among species and an increase in the diversity of habitats (and niches). In addition, flooding caused the valuable nutrients from the land to be washed away into the oceans, providing the building blocks for the development of shells and other hard parts that would give species a competitive edge in an increasingly predatory world. But sea level data suggest that it had been rising for millions and millions of years, beginning in the Precambrian Era, though this massive explosion of diversity is seen only at the very peak of the rising levels.

These questions are solved by understanding that in order to have an increase in speciation, and therefore in diversity, life itself must be "ready." Without multicellularity, for example, an increase in the availability of niches might not have been relevant, nor might there have been the availability of materials for constructing shells and other hard parts. As is often the case in biology, the "answer" to what is responsible for the Cambrian Explosion is likely a combination of these factors and several more. What is interesting to note is that once these major advancements had been achieved, the rate of the evolution of new innovations seems to also have increased (or, perhaps, though less likely, the fossil record becomes more accurate). You will notice that from now (550 mya) on, the time intervals describing big leaps in the story of the evolution of species will begin to decrease; changes are happening more rapidly.

There are several important advantages shared by organisms with exoskeletons: protection from the elements and predators, for example. Can you think of some disadvantages?

Fluffy on the outside, strong and rigid on the inside, there are several advantages to having an endoskeleton, including the ability to grow quickly.

A combination of conditions likely explains the increase in biodiversity marked in the fossil record during the Cambrian Period.

Lampreys are jawless fish that evolved perhaps 300 mya.

Vertebrates

The vertebrate body plan seems to have evolved only 400 my after multicellularity. This is remarkable given that the first multicellular organisms were essentially microscopic and the first vertebrate was a jawless fish, the ancestor of the sharks. A vertebrate is characterized by the presence of at least a back bone (in actuality, a series of bones),

though nowadays back bones usually come with a complete endoskeletal system (bones on the inside of the body). There are many advantages that are enjoyed by organisms that have an internal skeleton as opposed to an exoskeleton:

1) Growth can happen quickly without having to shed the exoskeleton and build it anew in a larger size.
2) Reproduction is much easier because the soft organs of the reproductive system can be easily accessed by the opposite sex.
3) Organisms can evolve the ability to move faster because of increased flexibility, range of motion, and a bit of a "spring" in cartilaginous tissues that keep bones together.

The first vertebrates were the jawless fish (Agnathids) and were similar to today's lampreys and hagfishes. With an absence of jaws, feeding is achieved by a strong suction cup–like mouth that attaches to the flesh of the prey. The teeth are moveable and they cut through the skin and muscle until body fluids such as blood are readily available for consumption. It is possible that this was also how some of the early jawless fish ate, though the very first ones were probably filter feeders that fed off of suspended plankton, much in the same way that oysters feed. The very early species of jawless fish appear to have maintained a thick exoskeleton of bony plates that were eventually lost while the endoskeleton became more elaborate and flexible.

Terrestrial Organisms

Though we often reference the transition from sea to land in common conversation (i.e. ". . . since we crawled out of the ocean"), determining when this event actually happened has proven to be difficult. In 2002, Dr. Simon Braddy and a team of paleontologists from the University of Bristol (United Kingdom) found fossilized footprints in ancient sand dunes in southeast Canada. The sandstone was dated to 530 mya and was part of the transition zone between marine and terrestrial environments, perhaps a tidal plane. It is unlikely that these footprints were made by an exclusively terrestrial organism. Instead, it is thought that the centipede-like creature used the terrestrial environment to either escape marine predators or to lay eggs like modern-day horseshoe crabs. Dr. Niedźwiedzki of Warsaw University and his colleagues published a research article in 2010 describing a series of fossilized footprints made by a *tetrapod* (four-legged animals with endoskeletons) and, because they were able to date those footprints to 395 mya, may represent some of the first vertebrates to walk the terrestrial environment. Though it is unclear which species is responsible for having made these tracks, it is certain that it had four limbs and digits (toes) rather than fins.

We can only really guess what the advantage of walking out on land presented to these enigmatic species. A few hypotheses have been described and, as before, the "correct answer" is likely some combination of all of them, depending upon

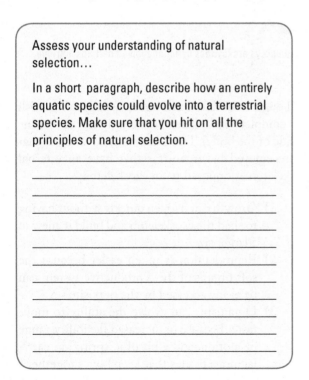

Assess your understanding of natural selection...

In a short paragraph, describe how an entirely aquatic species could evolve into a terrestrial species. Make sure that you hit on all the principles of natural selection.

_____
_____
_____
_____
_____
_____
_____
_____
_____
_____
_____
_____

© Andreas Meyer/Shutterstock.com

Eogyrinus sp., is a large tetrapod that lived both in the marine and terrestrial environments. It evolved during the Carboniferous period (360–300 mya) and therefore cannot be the species that made the footprints dated to 395 mya found in 2010, but could certainly have been similar.

the species and the limitations that they faced. The important question to ask yourself when you evaluate the validity of the hypothesis is: does this hypothesis describe a way that could increase the reproductive success of those individuals displaying that trait relative to those that do not? If the answer is yes, then you are perhaps on the right track.

One hypothesis states that marine organisms that could survive short periods of time in air were able to scavenge the intertidal zone (area of a beach that is bare during low tide and flooded during high tide) for stranded prey items. This would have given those individuals access to an abundant food resource with minimal competition and could have led to increased reproduction and the passing on of this trait to subsequent offspring. Similarly, escaping predators by "hiding" in air rather than in water would also be beneficial to survival and reproductive success. But we must be cautious when we explore these as reasons. Remember, there are a number of possible explanations and it is unlikely that only one applies.

The dinosaurs evolved about 235 mya. Their evolution does not represent a Paradigm Shift, per se, nor does it really describe a particularly important or diverse period on the planet. But they are included here because dinosaurs are cool. The first dinosaurs, however, were rather uncool. Imagine a large de-feathered chicken, a chicken with teeth, that is. In this case, it is Cope's law that was followed more closely than any other

© Marcio Jose Bastos Silva/Shutterstock.com

The first species of dinosaurs were rather small, bipedal, predatory creatures, measuring no more than 2 m in length.

terrestrial line: lineages of species tend to increase in body size throughout their evolutionary history. This is especially true with the herbivorous species. Some species reached body lengths in excess of 35 m and weighed over 50 tonnes. They represent the largest animals to have ever walked Earth. Presently, the largest dinosaur discovered was announced in September, 2014; a new species called *Dreadnoughtus* was estimated to weigh in at 60 tonnes and measure 26 m in length. One important exception has been noted to Cope's law: the predatory dinosaurs tended towards a more modest body that lead to the evolution of our modern-day birds.

The emblem species of the dinosaurs, *Tyrannosaurus rex,* arrived on the scene at the very end of the age of the dinosaurs: fossilized remains are dated only as far back as 68 mya. The most formidable and largest of all the land predators at the time, *T. Rex,* is referred to as an apex predator though it likely would not have passed up a meal of carrion. Measuring 4 m in height at the hip, and over 12 m long, this beast has often been depicted as a giant scaly lizard. But recent evidence supports the notion that *T. rex* had a fine layer of proto-feathers covering its body. Other species, including *Velociraptor,* were almost entirely covered in feathers.

But while the great (and the small) dinosaurs were wandering the Earth, wreaking havoc on both the vegetation and each other, something rather small and humble was evolving in the dark passages dug underground. The first mammals split off from the branches that led to the reptiles and birds about 320 mya and they lived throughout the time of the dinosaurs. In 2005, a 130-my-old fossil of a mammal known as *Repenomamus robustus* (about the size of a modern day opossum) was found with the skeleton of a juvenile *Psittacosaurus* (a bipedal herbivorous dinosaur about the size of a small deer at adult size) inside its stomach. Mammals are characterized largely by the presence of mammary glands (milk-producing organs) but there is little information available on the evolution of these structures because they do not preserve well in the fossil record. Thankfully, there are a couple of

The largest land animals to have ever evolved were herbivorous dinosaurs. Imagine this dinosaur to be *Dreadnoughtus*. Using any available resources, draw a person standing next to this dinosaur to scale.

© ExpressionImage/Shutterstock.com

© 3Dalia/Shutterstock.com

© Linda Bucklin/Shutterstock.com

Usually depicted as a scaly lizard-like creature (left), recent paleontological evidence shows that *Velociraptor* was covered in feathers (right).

other diagnostic tools that can be used to identify whether a fossil belongs to the mammals, including a reduction in the number of bones that comprise the jaw (mammals have only one bone in the lower jaw because the other bones evolved to be used in the inner ear), heterodont dentition (teeth of different shapes for different function), and the number of occipital condyles (protrusions at the base of the skull that form a contact with the first vertebra). Because these structures preserve well as fossils, they are used for identifying whether the species was a mammal rather than using the mammary glands.

Though there is increasing evidence that the early mammals were more diverse than previously thought, it is largely accepted that the first mammals were small bodied, large eyed, furry, insectivores at the mercy of the predatory dinosaurs. But there was not just a direct predator–prey relationship between early mammals

© CreativeNature R.Zwerver/Shutterstock.com

Like this shrew, the early mammals were small, furry insectivores that likely foraged only at night so as not to be eaten by dinosaurs.

and dinosaurs; they also competed for ecological niches and, until the extinction of the dinosaurs approximately 65 mya, the dinosaurs had been winning that competition. But then, about 66 mya, a giant asteroid collided with Earth that marked the end of the Cretaceous period and the beginning of the Cenozoic Era.

The idea that a space rock colliding with Earth was responsible for the extinction of the dinosaurs and approximately 75% of all the other species was not fully accepted by scientists until 2010. It was first proposed in 1980 by Dr. Luis Alvarez, a Nobel Prize–winning Physicist from the University of California, Berkeley, and his son, Dr. Walter Alvarez, a geologist at Berkeley. The two scientists analyzed the composition of an odd layer of clay that marks the extinction of the dinosaurs in the geological record. They found that the clay contains concentrations of iridium that are too high to have occurred naturally. Asteroids contain high concentrations of iridium and it did not take long for the Drs Alvarez to propose the origin. They did not know it at the time, but a giant crater, discovered in the late 1970s by two petroleum prospectors and geophysicists, Antonio Camargo and Glen Penfield, would support their hypothesis with more evidence. While searching for the next drilling site, Camargo and Penfield discovered an underwater arc in the topography 180 km in diameter. Subsequent calculations concluded that the asteroid responsible for making the crater was over 10 km in diameter with enough energy to produce an explosion 2 million times more powerful than the strongest explosion that humans have managed to produce thus far.

Try to imagine the consequences of such a collision; you will not be accused of exaggeration no matter how far into the catastrophic you go. Mega-tsunamis with wave heights in the order of hundreds, maybe thousands of metres and firestorms caused by the high concentration of oxygen in the atmosphere. The ash and debris released into the atmosphere blocked out the sun, rapidly killing off the plants, followed by the herbivores. But further up the food chain, the meat and insect eaters, there were fewer species extinctions; with an increase in available food (rotting herbivores, for example), and a decreased reliance upon the sun to live, those species able to survive the devastation of the actual meteor could have thrived. Up to 75% of the Earth's species went extinct as a result of that meteor, but one group of those that survived were essential to our evolution: the mammals.

Mammals

Without most of the dinosaurs around, mammals were no longer in an arms race for resources and with most niches now vacant they evolved, diversified, and spread over the globe. We currently have 5,500 species of mammals but estimates of past diversity suggest that there were a lot more at one time. The mammals can be divided up into five groups: volant, terrestrial, aquatic, fossorial, and arboreal, all of which occupy a diversity of niches. Before the crashing of a giant meteorite into the Yucatan Peninsula, dinosaurs occupied all of the niches now occupied by mammals, including fossorial!. It would have been unlikely that mammals could have evolved into these had they not first been vacated; competing with a dinosaur can be rough.

But even with the ecological advantage of massive devastation, it was a long time coming before *Homo sapiens sapiens* evolved: about 64.8 million years. Let us rewind and recap back to the beginning of mammalian diversification: the dinosaurs are dead, the mammals are underground, and a new paradigm has begun. The mammals at that time were adapted to a nocturnal, burrowing lifestyle and we can still see some of those ancestral traits in modern mammals. A keen sense of smell would have been advantageous for hunting at night. Large eyes would have gathered what little light was available. Endothermy (ability to regulate own body temperature without external sources of heat) and hair facilitated an active life in a cooler environment. And the ability to feed young from milk produced by the body would have

Assignment 10: Different teeth for different reasons

Name: _____   Student Number: _____

Look it up . . .

Most mammals have heterodont dentition (teeth with different shapes for different functions). Identify the different teeth for each of these jaws (dog, horse, and human), note the similarities and the differences in shape of the equivalent teeth. What might the function of each one be?

© Satirus/Shutterstock.com
© Satirus/Shutterstock.com
© aboikis/Shutterstock.com

1) Identify the different teeth for each of the above jaws (dog, horse, human)

2) What are the similarities among them?

_____

_____

3) What are the differences among them?

_____

_____

4) What is the function of each type of tooth?

_____

_____

5) Most mammals have heterodont dentition, but not all of them. What is a species of mammal that does not have heterodont dentition?

_____

_____

Marking:

1) Is the labelling correct?
2) Accurate similarities
3) Accurate differences
4) Accurate functions
5) Homodont dentition mammal

minimized predation of the offspring if they could be fed in underground dens. It is thought that these mammals were largely insectivores or omnivores and this helps us to understand why they survived the meteorite; an underground lifestyle combined with a diet that would not be immediately affected by the loss of plants (indeed, there would have been plenty to eat following the disaster) protected the mammals from extinction. Herbivorous mammals replaced the giant quadruped dinosaurs, active hunting carnivores with sharp teeth and claws now sported a coat of fur, and pterodactyls (though technically not dinosaurs but still affected by the meteorite) were replaced with bats (the second most diverse group of mammals).

A Reminder about Evolution by Natural Selection

As your mind's eyes try to imagine all of the story so far told, the giant meteorite and how it affected the entire planet, obliterating three quarters of its species, the emptiness that remained, and the diversification of the mammals, make sure that you do not fall back to imagine the details with some of the common misconceptions. For example, the opening up of vacant niches did not *cause* favourable mutations that allowed new species to occupy them. Rather, random mutations that happened to be favourable in the right context were selected, which eventually led to new species occupying new niches. Imagine a process that took millions of years, rather than a few generations; from a biological and geological perspective, a couple of million years is pretty quick.

Within a couple million years after the great meteor, there were hints at our eventual evolution, things that started to seem more human, looking back. *Carpolestes simpsoni*, a strange mouse-like tree-dwelling creature, evolved with grasping digits. Though reminiscent of a primate, it lacked forward-facing eyes, one of the diagnostic characters.

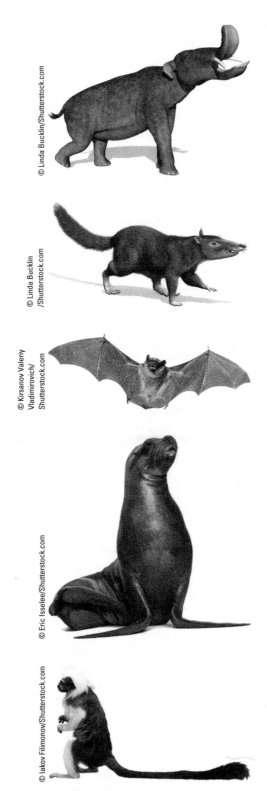

The diversification of mammals was facilitated by the extinction of the dinosaurs.

Primates

The primates, including humans, all share key diagnostic characters: forward-facing eyes, large brains protected by a domed cranium, opposable thumbs (though other groups also have this feature, e.g. opossums), short finger nails, and a reduced snout. It is still unclear exactly when primates first evolved but the best guess based upon fossil evidence from Morocco puts it at about 60 mya. This earliest known fossil record of a primate was published in 1990 by researchers out of the Université de Montpellier, France. Only 10 teeth were found but this is enough to identify the former owner as having been a primate. It is thought that based upon the size of the teeth, this first primate, *Altiatlasius koulchii*, weighed about 50–100 grams and was no bigger than a mouse lemur. Its discovery was significant not only for its age but also for its location; it cleared all the doubt about primates having been of African origin.

Though a diverse group ranging in size from the mouse lemur to the gorilla, the primates are characterized by having forward facing eyes, a large cranium to house the neocortex, keratin nails on each digit, a reduction of the olfactory regions of the brain and complex social behaviour.

Though there is still controversy regarding whether Ida, a fossil discovered in 1983 in Messel, Germany, represents a "missing" link between lemurs and "higher primates," there is little doubt that it is an excellent example of an early primate. Ida, the only known fossil of the species *Darwinius masillae*, dated at 47 million years old, was introduced to the world in 2009 after having been studied in secret by scientists for two years. It is a remarkably complete skeleton, with 95% of the bones accounted for, traces of hair and even her last meal: fruits and nuts. Such a significant find, however, was kept under wraps for over 20 years. The amateur fossil hunter, perhaps unaware of the significance, did not approach scientists at Oslo University's Natural History Museum until only recently and by that time knew enough to ask $USD 1,000,000. Ida died before reaching full maturity. This means that her baby teeth and her developing adult teeth are preserved. With a reduced snout, forward-facing eyes, and nails instead of claws, Ida was definitely a primate. And though at only 53 cm long she may have looked like a lemur, she was missing the two key characters: a grooming claw on her second toe and a fused set of teeth.

What is known about Ida's life is that she broke her wrist. Breaking her wrist did not kill her, for there is evidence of it having healed, but given her tree-dwelling lifestyle, it could have significantly decreased her ability to survive. Perhaps she was not as fast-moving or as agile. The area of Messel has so many well-preserved fossils that scientists think that the volcanic lake often filled with poisonous gases from underground rumbling, killing anything that fell into it. Ida's broken wrist could definitely account for her having become victim to a watery grave.

The first group of primates to diverge from the hominoid family was the gibbons. This event is thought to have occurred sometime between 15 and 20 mya. Therefore, we share with them the earliest ape ancestor. Apes are characterized by being tailless. The gibbons are unlike humans in every other respect; they have extremely long arms with a ball-and-socket joint in the wrists to support their arboreal lifestyle, tiny heads, and short legs.

Though Ida, discovered in Germany in 1983, may have looked like a lemur, she lacked the grooming claw (on second, or index, digit) that is characteristic of the group.

Not long after the divergence of the gibbons, there evolved the first great ape. These are large, tailless primates, with shoulder blades on their backs (rather than on their sides), gestation periods of eight to nine months and young that are relatively helpless for many years compared to other mammals.

Pierolapithecus

The oldest known fossilized great ape, *Pierolapithecus catalaunicus*, was found near Barcelona, Spain, in 2002 and it is thought to be 11.9 million years old. A reconstruction of the climatic conditions at the time suggests that this ancient ape lived in a warm, humid forest. The specimen itself, the only one ever found, is that of a male that weighed about 35 kg and fed on fruit. Examination of the fossilized remains has revealed that *Pierolapithecus* had a wider and flatter rib cage than monkeys and more importantly, a stiff lower back and wider pelvis. This may have allowed for a more stable vertical posture. But like the monkeys, *Pierolapithecus* had a sloped face and short fingers and toes. It is possible that this species is our common ancestor with the other great apes. It is also possible that it is not. What is certain is that this species represents the closest one to

Gibbons and humans share a very distance common ancestor that speciated approximately 15 mya.

our common ancestor found so far. The one thing that remains confusing is the location where the fossil remains were found: Spain. But all the other hominid species have been found in Africa. Examination of the topography of the Earth at the time of *Pierolapithecus* can easily explain the find: a contraction of the Mediterranean Sea facilitated the dispersal of organisms from Africa. It is therefore likely that many species were found on both continents.

Australopithecus

Prior to the discovery of *Pierolapithecus,* much attention was placed upon Lucy, the type specimen of *Australopithecus afarensis* first discovered in 1973 in Hadar, Ethiopia. Many characteristics make this hominid suggestive of humans: Lucy was bipedal, had thick enamel on the teeth, small canines, and grasping hands. Adaptations to the teeth since the evolution of *Pierolapithecus* include that the molars were taller, indicative of a diet composed primarily of vegetation (taller molars lasted wear-and-tear longer). But other characters are reminiscent of chimpanzees: Lucy was the size of chimpanzee with long arms, a forward-jutting jaw, and a small brain. Perhaps the most striking characteristic is that of having been bipedal (walking on two legs) and this discovery upset previous anthropological wisdom that supported the notion that large brains preceded walking. The Laetoli footprints in Tanzania, discovered in 1978, represent evidence of a bipedal hominid having walked across the volcanic ash 3.7 mya. A complete analysis of the footprints revealed that whoever left them may have been carrying something on the left side of their body, a baby perhaps. The stride pattern is remarkably similar to a human's; the heel hit the ground first followed by the ball of the foot to be pushed off with the toes for the next step.

Bipedalism

The evidence needed to diagnose bipedalism is unmistakable because a whole series of skeletal modification need to be present in order to facilitate walking upright. The head must be allowed to be held erect. The spine, therefore, must enter the base of the skull rather than the back. The difference is best understood by picturing a cat and then a human. The spine of the cat enters at

Two skulls belonging to the genus *Australopithecus*.

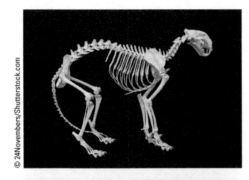

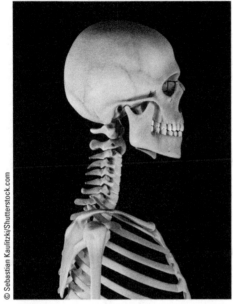

Adaptations to bipedalism begin with the skull. Here we appreciate the difference in the position of the spine relative to the skull between the cat, a quadruped, and a human, a biped.

the back of the skull so that the neck and back run parallel with the ground and the eyes and mouth are facing forward. If this configuration was present in humans we would all be looking at the sky. Our spine enters the base of our skulls so that our eyes and mouths are facing forward. The spine itself is shaped in a way that supports bipedalism; it is arched forward at the lumbar region (lower region of the spine) and it arches backward in the thoracic region (upper region of the spine). In this way, the body's centre of gravity is positioned above the feet and the spine is not tilted forward. The hip has adapted in many ways, including its orientation and its shape. The bones themselves are shorter and broader than the hip of a quadruped. This allowed for the evolution of larger gluteus muscles to provide greater support for upper half of the body, preventing it from pitching forward. The entire pelvis has shifted 90 degrees to face laterally, in line with the spine instead of facing downwards. The leg bones are significantly longer than those of quadrupeds. This takes advantage of the extended swing of the limb and allows for the trailing leg to be brought forward as a result of the distance between them rather than having to use muscle power to bring it forward. The femurs of bipedal hominids are angled inwards, towards the centre of the body axis to place the knees closer to the centre of gravity, allowing the knees to be locked, thereby reducing muscular effort to remain upright.

Finally, the arched foot is a dead giveaway: an extra robust heel absorbs the initial shock of each step and is then transmitted through the arch of the foot to the big toe.

But with often a lack of complete skeletons, identifying evidence of bipedalism can be challenging. For example, it is now thought that the earliest bipedal hominid (*Orrorin tugenensis*) evolved as early as 6 mya, though it likely spent much of its time in trees because it retained its long curved fingers, shorter legs, and longer arms. This was determined from a few teeth and two thigh bones found in 2000 by paleoanthropologists excavating in Kenya. It is not until *Homo erectus* evolved 1.9 mya that we see the complete "set" of bipedal adaptations, with long leg bones.

There is some debate regarding the reason for the evolution of bipedalism. We have all heard the various explanations. Bipedalism:

1) freed up the hands for tool use
2) allowed organisms to scan the horizon for predators or prey
3) restricted the sun's rays to only the head
4) was energetically less expensive

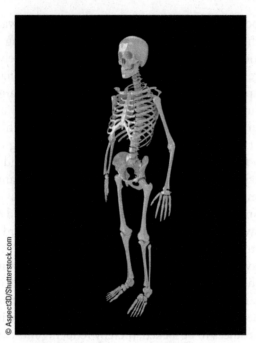

The curvatures of the spine reduce the energy necessary to maintain an upright posture.

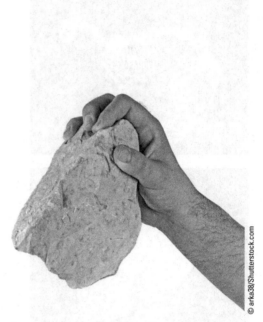

Some hypothesize that bipedalism evolved because it freed up the hands for tool use.

Darwin was a big supporter of the evolution of bipedalism for the freeing of hands for tool use. He wrote:

> "... the hands and arms could hardly have become perfect enough to have manufactured weapons, or to have hurled stones and spears with a true aim, as long as they were habitually used for locomotion."
>
> Charles Darwin The Descent of Man (1871)

Let us review...

So let us take this statement and write a hypothesis that can be tested.

Hypothesis: Bipedalism evolved because it allowed individuals to use tools.

If this is true, then we would expect to see supporting evidence. But what kind of evidence would convince us? How about:

Prediction: Evidence of tool use is found in geological proximity to bipedalism in the fossil record.

Label all of the adaptations to bipedalism that you can remember. Review the previous text and add in what you missed. Then search online for a few more that were not mentioned in the text.

Would that do it for you? What are the strengths of this prediction? What are the weaknesses?

A quick literature search reveals that the prediction is not supported: evidence of the most basic stone tool-use only shows up in the fossil record 4.5 million years after hominid bipedalism. That is a lot of time. Too much time. So moving on . . .

The next two hypotheses are somewhat related. Both of them suggest that whoever evolved bipedalism did so on an open savannah. There is indeed some supporting evidence if we look at climate data from around the time of the evolution of bipedalism. Generally, the climate was becoming drier and, as a result, parts of the forests that stretched across Africa were becoming patchy with open areas increasing in size. But this is not good enough to constitute definitive evidence. What is missing?

We would also have to see that the species that evolved bipedalism lived in that open savannah region. And this is where evidence is lacking. In fact, the evidence suggests that the first bipedal hominids lived in partially wooded areas.

What about the hypothesis that the skeletal adaptations for bipedalism require less energy for upright walking? This is a bit trickier. Who do we compare? And does it really address the issue of the advantage of walking upright? If you think about it, no, it does not. It only addresses the issue of if one is going to walk upright, one had better have the adaptations necessary to facilitate it.

Let us deal with this first.

Hypothesis: the adaptations required for bipedalism reduce the cost of locomotion.

Prediction: organisms without those adaptations will use more energy to walk upright than those that do. What are the strengths of this prediction? What are the weaknesses?

A study conducted in 2007 by Dr. David Raichlen at the University of Arizona measured exactly this. The researchers had five chimpanzees and four humans trained to walk on treadmills while they monitored their oxygen consumption (an proxy of energy consumption). Sure enough, the prediction was supported: chimpanzees use up

> *Extra questions to think about: Is this enough evidence to convince you that bipedalism did not evolve to free up the hands for tool use? What could confound the conclusion? What else would you need to be satisfied? Does that evidence exist?*

to 75% more energy to walk upright (or knuckle walk) than humans. No big surprise here because chimpanzees have to use a lot of muscle support to keep their naturally flexed joints from collapsing when walking upright, whereas humans propel themselves using the long rigid length of their leg bones. What was remarkable about the study though was that there was quite a bit of variation in the cost of walking upright among the chimpanzees: one chimpanzee named Lucy used significantly less oxygen on her treadmill walk. She also walked with straighter legs than the others.

What we have got now is one hypothesis, that walking upright with the adaptations requires less energy, and one supported prediction. Is this enough to convince you that the reason why bipedalism evolved was because it was energetically conservative?

The only thing that we can do is to consider other explanations and their plausibility. What could possibly be a better explanation?

How about: Hypothesis: Bipedalism evolved because it was a more efficient way for males to beat each other up while competing for females.

Prediction 1: Humans striking things from a quadruped posture will deliver less force than from a bipedal posture.

Prediction 2: Scientists will have way more fun doing this science experiment than others!

This experiment was carried out by Dr. David Carrier from the University of Utah and published in 2011. His prediction that striking force would be greater from a bipedal posture was indeed supported and this, coupled with the observations that many extant primate species regularly adopt a bipedal posture when engaging in violent competition for mates, seems to make this a plausible explanation. But is this really enough to evolve a complete transition to bipedalism? If apes adopt a bipedal posture in which to fight, is that not good enough?

If this is the case, then bipedalism evolved because of sexual selection due to mate competition.

So far there is not one accepted explanation for why bipedalism evolved. Nor does there really need to be because there are so many benefits and functions. Does it matter which benefit came first? And for such a complex trait with so many adaptations at multiple scales and across many biological systems, it makes sense that there would be so many possible explanations as to why it evolved in the first place; the answer is likely a bit of everything.

Back to *Australopithecus*

Though it was not the initial reason for the evolution of bipedalism, *Australopithecus*'s bipedal ability certainly allowed for the evolution of tool use. This was only recently discovered: a site in Dikika, Ethiopia, revealed bones with cut marks, evidence of butchering, dated to approximately 3.4 mya. The work was published in 2010 and, to date, the only hominid species found in that region is *Australopithecus afarensis*, the same species as Lucy. This makes it likely that *Australopithecus* was able to use tools. Tool use and meat eating are often associated concepts in the literature. It makes for a pretty logical and direct explanation for the usefulness of tool use. But though *Australopithecus* likely used tools to access calories in the form of meat, it is unlikely that their diet was composed largely of meat. Stable isotope analysis (a measure of the radioactive atoms used to form different tissues of the body) shows that the *Australopithecus* diet was composed primarily of plants related to the grasses, or animals that ate those grasses. Therefore, it is possible, if not likely, that *Australopithecus* ate animals such as lizards, birds, and small mammals but due to their limited cognitive ability and only very rudimentary tool kit, it is unlikely that they were able to compete against larger carnivores to hunt large game.

Many organisms have evolved bipedalism.

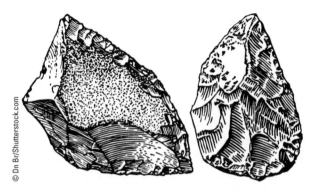

Though difficult to recognize by the untrained eye, early stone tools represent a major technological advancement in hominid evolution.

These recent discoveries present a challenge to the original paradigm that meat eating, tool use, and large brains are all connected and provide a positive feedback loop. The original argument goes like this: meat eating allowed for an increase in nutrient and calorie intake that allowed for larger brains to evolve, larger brains led to the evolution of stone tool making and food cooking, and stone tool making and food cooking allowed for more meat (and other foods) to be eaten.

The problem is that Lucy, and other Australopithecines, all had relatively small brains. Oh, and stone tool making predates cooking by a couple of million years. There is, however, evidence for a rapidly increasing brain size as cooked food became more prevalent in hominids. But this is only correlational data and there are other variables that plausibly contributed to the selection of larger brains, including the successful mastery of tools. The earliest evidence of controlled fire use is 1.0 million years old, at about the time of *Homo erectus*, and though this is not definitive proof of cooking, cooking food does raise its nutritional value and could therefore have supported the evolution of larger brains.

Oh the uncertainty of it all! Perhaps you are starting to question whether scientists really actually know anything. Perhaps you are wondering how we can talk about facts and truth with such questions remaining unanswered. I have always found that the more I learn about a scientific topic, the more I question the rigor of the methods. But

this is normal. And it really speaks to the wonder and beauty that is science. It not only can be used to acquire knowledge, but it can be used to stimulate creativity, to tap into our centres of curiosity and motivate us to keep on trying to answer questions. It is also important to note here that when we ask questions about events that occurred so long ago, we are generally asking some really difficult questions. Not all science is like this. Indeed, it is often less 'muddy' to describe something that is 'happening' (e.g. in a controlled experiment that you have set up and are executing) rather than something that has already happened, especially hundreds of thousands of years ago.

Homo Habilis

When the newly recognized species *Homo habilis* was announced to the scientific community, in 1964, the news was met with considerable scepticism. The type specimen, OH 7, was discovered by Louis Leakey and his team in 1960 in Olduvai Gorge, Tanzania. It consisted of a lower jaw bone with 13 teeth and 20 hand bone fragments. Several

Homo habilis was fully bipedal, capable of walking upright, but also spent time in the trees. This allowed them to survive the changing climatic conditions of the time.

Strong grasping hands are thought to be an adaptation to an arboreal lifestyle as seen here with orangutans. That *Homo habilis* had the strongest grasp of all *Homo* species suggests that it was able to exploit an arboreal environment.

criticisms were put forward by members of the scientific community. The bones were found in the region known to have supported a species of *Australopithecus* and many experts at the time did not think that the differences described in OH 7 were sufficiently great to warrant the naming of a new species. To accommodate the new species into the genus *Homo*, the previous definitions, including a larger braincase, needed to be relaxed. But, after much research it was accepted that the teeth, brain size, and shape of the hand were more similar to the genus *Homo* than *Australopithecus*, though it remains the most unlike humans in the genus. Not long after the discovery of OH 7, a foot was found nearby. It was originally thought to be from another individual because the fossil showed signs of arthritis. Arthritis is more commonly found in older individuals and based upon the size of the bones, OH 7 was not yet an adult at the time of death. However, after more research, it was determined that the arthritis was likely the result of a heeled injury and therefore it is probable that the foot belongs to the same individual.

Irrespective of the actual driver behind an increasing brain size, *Homo habilis* definitely had it; 500–800 cc compared to *Australopithecus* at no larger than 500 cc, yet still only half the brain size of

humans. Evolving on the grasslands and savannah of eastern Africa, there is evidence in the form of fossilized teeth to suggest that they handled a varied diet; an adaptation to unpredictable conditions that would have increased their resilience in a time of marked climatic change. Their teeth were smaller than *Australopithecus* and more akin to those of humans though they still had a thick layer of enamel and a stronger jaw that could process both soft fruits and animal tissue. They probably could not chew tough food like hard-shelled nuts as their ancestral species might have.

As for getting around the African savannah, a recent study conducted at the Johns Hopkins University School of Medicine by Dr. Christopher Ruff on bone strength of the limbs suggests that *Homo habilis* was indeed fully bipedal but also had the ability to spend time in trees. Curiously, and counter to what was thought previously, the grasping power in the hands of *Homo habilis* suggests that it was still able to interact in an arboreal environment (or, perhaps, had not yet lost that adaptation). It is not until *Homo erectus*, 1 million years later that a fully terrestrial hominid evolved.

Of note is the strong evidence for this species' reliance upon tools for the acquisition and preparation of food. The *Homo habilis* tool kit contained Oldowan tools: simple cores, retouched

Check it out . . .

Experimental anthropology is a field of study that focuses on the recreation of past activities to achieve functions relevant to human history.

You can watch some of these experiments online by searching for related videos.

See if you can find some and document which keywords brought you to the right place:

_____

_____

_____

_____

_____

A chimpanzee with a prodding stick used to get termites.

flakes, unretouched flakes, and flake fragments. Named by the Leakey family of archaeologists, the Oldowan tools are all those that are the oldest recognizable tools and therefore range in age from about 2.6 to 1.7 mya (though not until 0.5 mya in Europe).

Making a stone tool in the Oldowan style is not terribly complicated on paper though it takes some time to develop the practical skills required. That, or a lot of trial and error. A hammerstone, spherical in shape, is struck against a core stone to produce a sharp-edged flake that is the piece removed from the core. The flakes were often not retouched to be made sharper or into a desired shape, so it can be difficult to distinguish a flake from just a broken rock. Intensive studies by archaeologists who investigated the tool-making techniques have now made the identification of such deliberately created pieces more reliable. These newly made tools were then used in various ways—cutting, scraping, piercing, grinding of animal and plant tissue—and the resulting microscopic wear markings were compared with those of ancient tools. In this way, the uses of each of the tools were determined. There were choppers with one sharp edge, scrapers for stripping flesh from hide and bone, awls for boring holes, and burins for engraving.

At the time that *Homo habilis* lived, it is likely that there were at least four other hominid species living. There is evidence to suggest that they did not each occupy separate parts of the globe but overlapped in range. Imagine what it would be like today if another species of the genus *Homo* lived among us. Would we get along just fine? Would we be enemies? Would we segregate ourselves? There was likely some competition for resources but it appears as though *Homo habilis* was the most able to make and wield complex tools used primarily to access a wider variety of food resources. It is still unclear whether *Homo habilis* is the common ancestor of the genus *Homo* or whether it is another *Homo* species with which we share a common ancestor. Irrespective of which is correct (and we may never know the answer), the species seems to have succeeded in surviving and it is likely due to its relatively advanced technology.

Studies of tool technology have been used to deduce the lifestyle and cognitive abilities of the species. For example, the discovery of shape flakes in association with the bones of *Homo habilis* has been used to suggest that they butchered meat, rather than simply eating what they could access with their hands alone.

It is important to note one very important caveat in interpreting the association of bones and tools; resource availability can vary over the landscape. It is known that, for example, the size of the stones used for tool making does not have a uniform distribution. This means that some areas are rich in a resource while others are without that resource entirely. Therefore, in some regions larger stones are more readily available. Larger stones tend to allow for a greater diversity of tools with a greater diversity of uses. If the raw materials are not available, then the tool cannot be made. It is not an indication of a lack of cognitive abilities of that species. Interestingly, information about the distribution of raw materials can be used to infer whether the tool found was used where it was made and then discarded or whether it was carried around in a tool kit. Chimpanzees do not carry tools around. They fashion them with local resources and use them as "disposable" items to meet immediate needs. For example, chimpanzees use sticks from the *Grewia* plant to probe for termites. Because they do not carry around a probe once it has been made, areas with greater densities of *Grewia* tend to have chimpanzees that feed on termites. Conversely, the discovery of tools in areas where the raw materials for making them are not found is an indication that they were carried around, as personal possessions. This is the case with several *Homo habilis* archaeological sites; tools made from raw materials that are not found in the region were discovered. And so, it seems that with *Homo habilis*, though the actual use of tools may have evolved earlier, the tool box most likely evolved with this species.

Homo Sapiens

And so here we are. Human beings, the epitome of cognition, the thinking person. Will it bother you to learn that we, human beings or at least the ones living upon the planet today, are actually likely to be a "subspecies." We are *Homo sapiens sapiens*, the thinking *thinking* people. And if we are a subspecies, then it means that there must be at least one other. One with which we share 99.5% of our DNA. Please do not start looking around the room for members of this other subspecies. And no, your sister is not "one of them." The other subspecies is the Neanderthal, *Homo sapiens neanderthalensis*. Maybe. It could also be *Homo sapiens idaltu*, but we are going to stick to Neanderthals.

So before we move on, let us recognize that what I have said may be a bit controversial outside of the field of biology. Does it bother you that Neanderthal is now classified as another type of human? What are the implications? Indeed, what is implied? Well, if we use the biological species concept, what is implied is that Neanderthal and humans are capable of producing viable offspring. And, indeed, it appears as though this was occasionally "tested" in nature. A recent paper, published in 2010 by a large group of scientists from both North America and Europe, has demonstrated that a small percentage (approximately 62,000 base pairs, or 4%) of the modern human genome of European descent is derived from the Neanderthal genome. Though there are several ways in which genomes can be mixed around nowadays, there was really only one way over 30,000 years ago: sexual reproduction.

In many cases it would be very difficult to identify a Neanderthal walking amongst a group of *Homo sapiens sapiens*.

Given that it is rather likely that humans migrating into Europe interbred with the Neanderthals living there, aren't you glad that Neanderthals are now recognized as having been human also? So indeed, if your ancestors are of European descent, it is likely that you have got a little Neanderthal in you.

And those of you reading this text thinking, "well, I'm of Asian descent, so I'm pure *Homo sapiens sapiens*", I say "bzzzzzt" to you. It is likely that the human migrants who went through southern Asia also interbred with the local human subspecies that occupied those regions. They are called the Denisovans.

Homo Sapiens Neanderthalensis

Unlike some of the other hominid species, a lot of Neanderthal bones have been found. Over 400 individuals have been dug up, the first in 1856 in

Neandertal, Germany (actually, the first one was discovered in Belgium in 1829 but it was not recognized as something extra special). The timing of this discovery was important; it was three years before Darwin's *On the Origin of Species*. When that publication came out, readers could not help but make connections to the Neanderthal discovery and its implications.

Though no one is quite sure, it is thought that Neanderthals evolved over 500,000 years ago. The oldest fossils are only about 200,000 years old however, and their abundance is because Neanderthals buried their dead. Burial increases the likelihood of fossilization. The many fossils discovered span enough of the range to be able to demonstrate that the oldest fossils more closely resembled the earlier hominids while the younger fossils are more human-like. What comes to mind when we think "Neanderthal" did not evolve until about 70,000 years ago. On average, Neanderthal was slightly shorter than modern humans and quite a bit stockier in build. It is thought that this represents an adaptive advantage in colder climates, though there is some criticism of this conclusion and the counter-suggestion that the Neanderthal body represents an adaptation to close-proximity hunting strategies. Neanderthal also had a larger brain, straighter hair, and lighter skin. Given the climate at the time their tools, and isotopic analysis of their bones, it is thought that they relied heavily on a diet of meat that was only supplemented by vegetation. Recent evidence suggests that the vegetation in their diets consisted of roots, nuts, and berries. Analyses of their bones have shown that they suffered frequent bone fractures consistent with those sustained by rodeo cowboys! This suggests that they regularly interacted with large animals. Their arms demonstrated left–right symmetry suggesting that they took down prey at close proximity using thrusting spears rather than throwing weapons. (Because spears are usually launched with the same arm, an asymmetry would likely develop over time.) Those individuals living near coasts were able to exploit marine resources such as fish. It has been determined that Neanderthal possessed fire-controlling

technology and likely cooked food regularly in addition to preparing medicines and building shelters.

It is difficult to describe the Neanderthal niche in a paragraph or two. This is because their distribution was scattered across Europe. From Israel, to Gibraltar, to Northern Germany, Neanderthal inhabited a variety of ecosystems and all evidence suggests that they were well suited to survive and thrive within them. Those that lived near the coasts adopted a maritime lifestyle, fishing and scavenging small marine mammals, and making dugout boats to explore areas of the Mediterranean Sea. Those that lived in the mountains fed primarily on small mammals such as rabbits but also took deer and larger animals when the opportunity presented itself. And throughout the populations, vegetation was present in the diet.

The Neanderthal tool kit was a Mousterian kit with stone flakes, hand axes, spears, and knives. The Mousterian technology represents a revolution in tool making. It is a progression in efficient use of materials; rather than chipping away at a good stone to make one tool, Mousterian tools were removed from a desired stone so that several tools could be fashioned.

At first glance, all of this speaks of a highly intelligent and cultured species with the ability to think in abstraction. Art is said to represent the storage of information outside of the brain and is evidence of culture. Similarly, in a cave in Iraq, the bodies of individual Neanderthals were found to have been buried with ornamental flowers and tools. But often we tend to over-interpret these findings in our desire to connect with past species. In a cautionary paper by Jeffrey Sommer, from the Museum of Anthropology at the University of Michigan, the finding of ornamental flower pollen at the grave sites of some Neanderthals in Iraq can be explained by the burrowing behaviour of a local rodent. This, of course, does not mean that Neanderthals did not intentionally bury their dead, nor does it suggest that they did not have the cognitive abilities similar to those of *Homo sapiens sapiens*. It simply means that finding pollen around the bones may not be the conclusive evidence of those things. But, irrespective of

Assignment 11: So many Neanderthals

Name: _____   Student Number: _____

Think about it . . .

Unlike other species from the genus *Homo*, many more Neanderthal skeletons have been found. What are three plausible hypotheses that could explain this?

1) _____

_____

_____

_____

_____

2) _____

_____

_____

_____

_____

3) _____

_____

_____

_____

_____

Marking:

1) Are the hypotheses actually hypotheses?

2) Are the hypotheses plausible?

whether the burials were decorated with flowers, the Neanderthals of the Shanidar Caves provide an unprecedented amount of information regarding their natural history. One of the skeletons in particular is remarkable because of its deformity. Shanidar 1, so the body is creatively called, suffered quite a blow to the side of his head that likely left him blind in one eye. It is known that the blow did not kill him because the wounds had healed. The injury also left him paralyzed on one side; his right arm bone is withered from lack of use. Shanidar 1 would not have been able to survive on his own having sustained such an injury. He must have been cared for by others, his family perhaps. And though "caring for others" is not unique in the natural world, it certainly includes a rather limited group.

With all of this technology and civilization, it is not illogical to think that Neanderthals got on by speaking with each other. Surely they must have had language. Well, it is not an easy task to prove this definitively from the evidence and samples that are available. At first it was thought that possession of the FOXP2 variant of a certain gene was proof positive of the trait called "language." It turns out that it is not quite that simple.

FOXP2 is a gene that has been identified to play an important role in the development of language and speech skills in humans in addition to contributing to brain neural connection development. Humans that have mutations of the *FOXP2* gene exhibit severe speech disorder. *FOXP2* is also found in other animals including chimpanzees, mice, songbirds, and elephants. However, two mutations have been found that exist only in the human line of the *FOXP2* gene. Both *Homo sapiens sapiens* and *Homo sapiens neanderthalensis* possess these two mutations. This suggests that it arose in at least the common ancestor of the two subspecies. But recently it has been found that

bats possess
it has been
FOXP2
comm
allov
th

i
both mo
about 500,0
divergence betwe
tion event has been d
One of the first propos
may in fact be human came
Director of the Moravian Museu
mer Czechoslovakia in 1969. His a
published along with 10 reviews by pron
scientists in the field at the time. He used mo
phometric measures to argue that the variation found in the Neanderthal bones fell within the range of those measures in humans. Since this time anthropologists have been debating the question back and forth using different means of analysis including genetic testing. Recently, DNA analyses of both Neanderthal and human showed so little difference between them that, using genetic information alone, they could be considered to be of the same species. And the most recent findings of hybridization seem to end the debate. But not so. It has been suggested that the only fertile offspring of a Neanderthal/ Human cross were female, and genetic evidence suggests that only a cross between male Neanderthals and female humans was able to produce viable female offspring. Comparison of the mitochondrial DNA, genetic information passed on only along the matrilineal line, supports this hypothesis. If this is the case, then would we really consider them to be the same species? The question is still being debated in the literature and I am certain that within the next few years further exciting evidence will be presented.

Homo sapiens sapiens

Homo sapiens, the thinking man, human. This Latin name was coined by Carolus Linneaus and it is recognized as having been named in 1758, along with about 10,000 other species, 6,000 of which were plants. This, however, is not entirely accurate because the 1758 version of his taxonomy was actually the 10th edition. Many of these names were published in previous editions. Though many of the classifications made by Linneaus in this landmark publication proved to be incorrect (for example, he had a whole section on minerals), remarkable at that time was his classification of humans in the same group as the other primates: Anthropomorpha. Recognizing that this could be rather controversial, Linneaus had the following to say:

> *"It does not please [you] that I've placed Man among the Anthropomorpha, perhaps because of the term 'with human form', but man learns to know himself. Let's not quibble over words. It will be the same to me whatever name we apply. But I seek from you and from the whole world a generic difference between man and simian that [follows] from the principles of Natural History. I absolutely know of none. If only someone might tell me a single one! If I would have called man a simian or vice versa, I would have brought together all the theologians against me. Perhaps I ought to have by virtue of the law of the discipline."*

(Linneaus, 1747)

Carolus Linneaus, 1707–1778.

© Georgios Kollidas/Shutterstock.com

It is remarkable because this line of thinking, about the relationship between primates and humans, comes more than 100 years *before* Darwin's even more controversial text, but Linneaus acknowledges the implication and the assault that it will represent to theologians!

In his description of *Homo sapiens sapiens*, Linneaus used only his own body as reference. For this reason, and, I assume, for his great contribution to biology, his body remains as the "type specimen" of humanity.

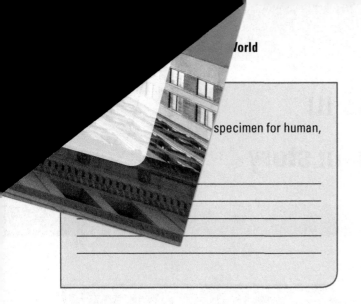

specimen for human,

How to Recognize a Human

The identification of humans may come off as being rather easy but, actually, there are really only some rather subtle distinctions, morphologically speaking, that characterize us. Imagine that you are texting with an alien. The alien asks: "so what do you look like?" What might you say?

Humans are bipedal. Walking on two of our four appendages is definitely a species characteristic. We have many adjustments to our bodies from the original quadruped body plan that allow for and facilitate this type of locomotion. Our spine enters our skull at its base rather than back, our hips are rotated and shifted, our spine is S-shaped, and we have arched feet (see chapter on evolution for more details). We are terrestrial bipeds, meaning that we occupy the part of the Earth that is land, and though we can swim and dive, we do so relatively poorly.

Human have large brains. Our brains are so large that it was once thought that the reason we are born so helpless and underdeveloped is because if we were to gestate any longer inside our mothers, our heads would be too big to pass through the birth canal. Now, this has since been shown to be an unlikely explanation; human gestation is rather long, and human babies are double the size of what would be predicted from adult body size compared with other primates. Though our brains are only 30% of adult size at birth compared with 40% for chimpanzees, a human female pelvis would only need to be about 2 cm wider to accommodate a chimpanzee-brain–equivalent baby. This small value is well within the natural variation that exists in human female pelvises. It turns out that our gestation length has more to do with hitting a point where the mother is just not able to give more of her body energy to the baby. But our brains are indeed very large, larger than predicted by our body size. And though some animals also have larger than predicted brains, we stand out on top. Some of the other "brainy" animals include chimpanzees, dolphins, foxes, cats, and, to my delight: the echidna!

Think about it . . .

How could you "show" that the variation among humans in weaning age has a lot more variation than other mammals? Try to depict it in the space provided. Test it out by asking someone else to tell you what you have drawn.

The human brain is not all that different from those of other mammals; all the basic structures are the same. However, our brains have parts that are larger relative to other parts. The larger bits are mostly associated with abstract thought processing, reasoning, planning, language, and vision. This region of the brain is referred to as the neocortex and it is the largest part of the cerebral cortex, representing over 90% of the brain in humans.

We touched a bit earlier on gestation period and I commented on it being rather long relative to most other mammals (the opossum, for example, has a gestation period of only 14 days but the elephant goes 23 months). Indeed, this is one of the characteristics of humans; it takes us a long time to reach maturity. Not only do we have a long gestation (about 40 weeks), but we also have a very long period of infancy. Weaning is what marks the end of infancy and the beginning of childhood. Giraffes, for random example, are weaned by about

1 month old and reach full maturity by 4 years. Mice are weaned by 3 weeks old and reach maturity at 2 months. What about humans? Well, there is quite a bit of variation in the time to weaning and much of it depends upon geography. In some places, weaning happens as late as age 5, even 6, and people in other places wean their children off milk after only a few months. The median age of human weaning is probably somewhere between 2 and 3 years. Studies on breastfeeding in human babies have suggested that weaning should take place no earlier than 2.5 years but could be extended up to 7 years. Interestingly, many cultures do not support this "extended" period of breastfeeding and in some cases, women have been accused of inappropriate contact with their child for nursing them as young as 1 year old.

There are several hypotheses related to the extended human ontogeny (period from conception to adulthood) and are generally related to the need

Pheasants have a great deal of sexual dimorphism, shown here with the female (left) and male (right) common pheasant.

to develop "plastic" responses to environmental stimuli and to learn rather complex social norms and appropriate interactions. Most of the behaviours in which we need to engage to survive must be learned, and with our rather complex cultural systems, the list of things that we need to learn and the behaviours that we need to perfect continues to grow. We can also note here that some behaviours, once very important, are no longer required for our survival. Can you think of a few?

Humans display relatively little sexual dimorphism (differences between the sexes). Though our culture tends to place great importance (and also humour) on the differences between men and women, relative to other species in the animal kingdom, we are not that different from each other.

On the issue of strength between men and women, it is not so clear cut. Surely you can appreciate that the strongest woman is stronger than the weakest man; there is overlap. This is because though there is a statistical difference between men and women strength, both respond almost equally, respective to their body size, to training. In fact, much of the difference noted between males and females with respect to physical performance can be explained by natural differences in body composition; women tend to have a greater percent body fat than men. When high endurance athletes are studied, people who have similar measures of percent body fat, sex is eliminated as a significant variable to describe any difference in performance. That is, there is not as much difference in physical performance as we might think.

There are, of course, some differences. Women tend to have better immune systems; they are better able to fight infection and recover from trauma. Recent studies by scientists in Belgium have shown that this may be linked to DNA on the X-chromosome, of which women have two and men have one. Women also live longer by approximately five years in Canada though this gap has been decreasing.

Within the brain there are several differences between men and women. A 2005 study from the University of California, Irvine, found that women have more white matter and men have more grey matter associated with their intelligence and that

overall, there was no measurable difference in intelligence.

But a 2015 study from the University of Pennsylvania found that women have a higher percentage of grey matter when compared with men. In addition, they found that there were more neural connections between the left and right hemispheres in women and more connections between the fore and hind brain in men. Clearly more research is required to further identify differences though it appears as though these differences really only speak to the possibility of achieving similar functionality in a variety of ways. As with body strength, there is great overlap between the sexes and a great many individual exceptions.

But most of our perceivable differences have to do with our primary (the sex organs themselves) and secondary sexual characteristics including male facial and Adam's apple and female breasts. And even then there is often great overlap (e.g. breast size).

So we come back to our conversation with an alien and we say "humans are bipedal, big brained, slow to grow, and similar between the sexes." Does the alien find it easy to picture a human? Might it confuse us with a chimpanzee? Or an albatross? And so you need to continue talking, adding things that distinguish us from other species. And then, perhaps, you realize that it is in your ability to talk that holds the key to distinguish us from other animals: humans have language!

For all of the differences that we associate with the sexes, many of them overlap and all of them are considerably smaller than in other species.

Humpback whales are known for their long and individually unique songs.

Language is an incredible technology. It serves as a "remote control" whereby I could simply say "please pass the salt" and, without delay, a shaker of salt comes my way brought to me by someone else. This is indeed incredibly powerful and even before babies can speak they learn that a simple cry will bring them all that they need and, often, more! But are we the only species that has this trait? This is where it gets murky. There are not any organisms that have not evolved a mechanism for communication in some way. Granted, some of the communications appear to be rather simplistic (e.g. chemical communication through the production of pheromones) and not really what we are getting at. But what about the songs of birds or humpback whales? Can these be considered language? There are a few things that we must consider.

Our communications are complex. And though this does not make them "unique," they are certainly more complex than the next most complex communication system. Consider the song of a humpback whale. Within the song there are distinct phrases and themes that are repeated, sometimes for days. The phrases change over time as the whale ages and each whale's song is slightly different. Much of the singing is done by males during the reproduction season and so it is thought that the song is meant to attract mates. If we take a look at the "base unit" of the song, a note, and compare this with our base unit, a syllable, there are some important differences. The first being that we can form far more distinct syllables than whales can notes. But that is perhaps rather trivial. The most important distinction is that we can pack more syllables into a specific time period than can whales. Whale notes last up to a few seconds each. Syllables are short and sweet. So we say that human language has more "bits" per second than other forms of communication.

Another feature of human language is that it is modality-independent. This means that meaning can be transmitted in various forms without the loss of information. Bees are able to give flying directions to other bees by means of a dance. However, an injured bee that cannot dance is not capable of giving directions. Much of the time, we communicate by speaking and listening to each other. There are some people that are unable to hear but this does not mean that they are exempt from communicating. Language can be transmitted in written or hand gesture form as well. The means by which the message is transmitted is independent of the message.

Finally, language allows for abstract thought, planning, and reminiscing. To date, these features have not been identified in other communication systems in other species. And how human language came to be is still largely under debate. It seems unlikely that there was some "switch" that evolved in the brain to allow us to make complex sentences about the past or the future (though some linguists argue that this is indeed what happened). A whole suite of anatomical modifications were required in order to allow for the diversity and rapidity of sound

Look it up . . .

Many marine species make some rather surprising sounds. Spend some time online searching for recordings of the following animals:

- Bearded seal
- Snapping shrimp
- Northern seahorse

Sign language represents a different modality of language delivery, not a different language.

production, in addition to the brain power to be able to appreciate different tenses. It is unlikely that we are, therefore, the first species to have this ability given the long line of hominids before us. Many anthropologists, for example, believe quite convincingly that Neanderthals had language, similar to how we know it today. But the evidence for just how far back it goes is shaky at best. What would we look for? What find would convince you that a species had language? The anatomy has to be right. This is perhaps the easiest part. Then we might look for signs of culture, evidence of complex behaviours that require planning, technology that uses resources from faraway places, right and left brain separation of function. All of these have been used to argue in favour of Neanderthal language systems.

And so language may not have been able to identify *Homo sapiens sapiens* had these aliens visited 50,000 years ago, but it certainly helps now.

Perhaps in this description, another word came to mind: culture. It has been suggested that language is what allowed for culture as an adaptive mechanism to evolve. But this term is even more loaded than "language" and even more difficult to define. We may be able to inherently identify aspects of culture but devising a definition that encompasses all aspects and nuances is a toughy. The word's first usage occurred with

the publication of the book *Primitive Culture* by anthropologist Edward Tylor, of England, in 1871. Tylor fell into the field of anthropology before it really existed. At the age of 23, his doctor recommended moving to a warmer climate to recover from tuberculosis and so Tylor moved to Mexico. His first book on the subject of its people, past and present, was published in 1861. Tylor became Oxford University's first professor of anthropology. He had never even gone to university. In his 1871 book on the subject of culture, Tylor defines it as "..that complex whole which includes knowledge, belief, art, morals, law, custom, and any other capabilities and habits acquired by man [sic] as a member of society." This, for our purposes, and for the appeasement of those evolutionary psychologists upset with the willy-nilly use of the term by social scientists, should be boiled down further into something like "the full range of learned human behavioural patterns."

It is not our ability to learn behavioural patterns that makes us unique. Indeed, there are animals that learn behaviours from their parents or social groups. Rather, it is the complexity of our behavioural patterns and the number of them that we have to learn that sets us apart. Songbirds, for example, learn their song by hearing adults sing. It is known that should a bird reach maturity in isolation from others of its species, it will sing, but it will sing a rather odd song that will not be effective in attracting mates.

Songbirds need to learn their song by listening to adults of their species.

But compared to the behaviours in which humans need to engage in order to attract a mate (indeed, some humans never learn!), singing a song, no matter how complex, in the springtime is relatively simple.

For a behaviour to become "culture," a few key elements are required. Without all of them, the behaviour is not likely to become part of the human culture. With the invention of a new behaviour, these requirements are consistency among performers, permanence in the performer, spatial transmission, and temporal transmission.

> *Permanence in the performer*: The same individual must be able to reliably repeat the same behaviour to the same effect. A baker who cannot repeat the same recipe for bread may find that she loses her customers rather quickly. For a behaviour to be maintained in culture, it must be repeatable.
>
> *Consistency among performers*: Different individuals need to be able to perform the same behaviour in the same way so that the function is maintained. The behaviours required to successfully sew, for example, are simple and can be accomplished by any person. Though often these behaviours can be performed with increasing skill, the basics can be performed by enough individuals in the population to be maintained.

Behaviours must be temporally transmitted in order to be considered "culture."

> *Spatial transmission*: The behaviour in question must "travel" across space. This is usually done by one person observing another performing the act, or a person telling another about it in a way that makes it repeatable elsewhere. The use of the hula-hoop has been around for hundreds of years. But in 1958 its popularity spread like a disease outbreak when a plastic version was mass produced. Within a year, people, children especially, were hula-hooping across America.
>
> *Temporal transmission*: Time is an important barrier to the development of culture. The behaviour must be passed on to subsequent generations. The generational gap is also a convenient "opportunity" to get rid of certain behaviours such as the wearing of bell bottom pants, or, hopefully in the future, skinny jeans.

So what sets us, *Homo sapiens sapiens*, apart from other organisms, is not necessarily that they do not have culture as it is defined here, but rather that, if they do have aspects of culture, it is not nearly as complex. It is hoped that you can appreciate that we are balancing on some rather fine filaments that could snap with disciplinary dogma. And this, to some degree, is the point. It is difficult to describe humans outside of the natural world and apart from the evolutionary tree that holds common ancestors and closely related species.

But there is one last aspect to explore: that of niche. Remember? We have already talked lots about niche, the roles that species play in the complex web that is the ecosystem. We have carnivores and decomposers, prey, and primary producers that take carbon dioxide and make oxygen. In your answer to the alien question, as a last resort, you might add that *Homo sapiens sapiens* is the only species with the ability to adapt the environment to change its niche rather than adapting to it. After all, the ultimate consequence of all the above-mentioned human traits is that we do not need to suffer and physically adapt to nature's randomness anymore, because

Grasslands are very fertile ecosystems, but over time they can transform into forests if the frequency of fire is not high enough to kill germinating trees and shrubs. Prescribed burning to maintain grassland ecosystems has been performed by human societies for thousands of years. Now prescribed burnings are used in most grassland national parks. Early niche construction by humans therefore left us with a culturally tainted natural heritage that we strive to protect, but it put into question the notion of "pristine" or "virgin" environment. Do you think we should let ecosystems change on their own without interventions? Or are humans part of the natural change that happens?

we can rationalize problems with our brain, discuss them with our language, and use our tools to fix the issue and modify our environment in order to maintain our "quality" of life. If a forest does not meet our needs, we can burn it to create farming lands, and if the winter is too cold, no need to evolve fur over generations of time when you can build a house and control fire! This capacity of a species is known as niche construction, and refers to the ability of species to build new niches, whether for itself or other species. In this context, niche construction, although well developed and used by humans, is also performed, to a smaller degree by many other species. Trees create forests, ants farm aphids and mushrooms, and beavers create ponds.

Therefore, when you are asked by an alien, "what is human?", it is perhaps best to describe all the things that we have presented and then cap it off with "there is not really one thing that is unique to humans, humanity is not necessarily the invention of anything, but rather the improvement of many." Or perhaps, if you meet an alien, you should run.

And so, approximately 200,000 years ago, *Homo sapiens sapiens* evolved and, like evolution itself, change was slow at first as new paradigms were introduced that were then exploited for increasingly rapid adaptation. All evidence points to Africa as the continent of origin with the oldest human fossil found so far coming from Ethiopia and recently dated to 195,000 years old. Discovered in 1967, it was thought to have been 130,000 years old but a reanalysis in 2005 using more modern techniques increased the age considerably.

Cities are a unique human-created ecosystem that opened new niches for a wide range of species. Urban ecologists are the scientists that only recently started to investigate the complexity of this novel ecosystem previously perceived as an area depleted of life. Urban ecology redefines our perception of human impact on the planet by illustrating that many species strongly benefit from our new urban ecosystems.

Your time budget…

Fill in the first pie chart to describe how you spend your day. How much time do you spend eating? Sleeping? Studying? Working on non-school–related things? Playing?

1)

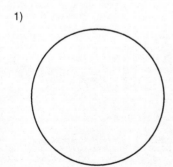

2)

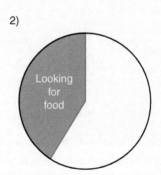

Looking for food

Fill in the second pie chart imagining that you were an early human hunter-gatherer. How would you spend the rest of your time?

But there is a competing hypothesis by scientists from three major research medical schools in the USA. They claim that humans evolved while feeding on catfish, shellfish, crustaceans (shrimp, lobster), cephalopods (squid and octopus), sea urchins, and amphibians, birds and reptiles associated with the marine and freshwater habitats of Africa. The scientists suggest that it is because of these foods' high concentrations of an important fatty acid (docosahexaenoic acid, DHA) that the brains of humans were able to become three times larger than their ancestors' when correcting for differences in body mass. They suggest that it is because of their reliance upon the marine and freshwater ecosystems as a source of DHA that humans were forced to remain close to them. The scientists making this claim account for a lack of fishing tool evidence by determining that it would not be necessary to develop special technology to acquire these resources. It is not until 90,000 years ago that there is evidence that fishing tools were being made. The scientists go on to say that a mutation in the human genome allowed for better digestion and more efficient use of plant material and that this, ultimately, facilitated the great human migration out of Africa by allowing humans to wander further from their energy-rich marine and freshwater food sources. They tested this hypothesis by looking at modern human genomes and found some interesting, though not conclusive, correlations.

Though this study is not widely cited, it is interesting to think about the possibility that our assumptions that humans evolved as staunch meat eaters may not be entirely accurate. The study suggests that humans had a different niche than the one we assume. What further evidence would we need to find in order to support their hypothesis? How could we test it?

There is a lot of evidence supporting the notion that early humans were capable of hunting large mammals. Evidence has also been found, primarily in the region now known as Belgium, to support the hypothesis that Neanderthals regularly hunted large mammals like the mammoth. It seems unlikely that humans would not have been able to do the same. And so given these two possibilities, we have two very different niches characterizing early humans. As more evidence is found, supporting either side, or even perhaps a completely different interpretation, the story will continue to unfold.

It has been mentioned before that we are capable of changing our environment to change our niche. And what is more remarkable, and certainly more unlike any other species (for it seems plausible that other species have also

There is some debate over when humans began to exploit the marine and freshwater ecosystems. Some think that it was necessary in order to allow for an increase in brain size, others think that it happened only after the invention of fishing tools, perhaps as late as 90,000 years ago.

The Bajau Laut are a marine adapted population, building their homes on stilts in the ocean.

experienced niche changes over time), is that the human niche is so variable spatially and, if you want to "zoom in" further, you could argue that within a population, different humans have different niches. There is a lot of variation. That is to say, our niche is different depending upon where we are and maybe even who we are.

The Bajau Laut live on the waters between the Philippines and Indonesia, often several kilometres from land. They have built their homes on stilts embedded into the coral reefs and have evolved to live successfully off the resources of the ocean. Some spend so much time at sea that they claim to become ill when they set foot ashore. Landsick! The only resources acquired from the land are rice and fuel for their boats. Imagine living your life on the sea without touching land. Imagine that you had a completely different tool kit to work with. Imagine what you would eat. Imagine how you would find fresh water, shelter, warmth, clothing, everything that you need to survive and thrive on a watery world.

The Inuit of Canada also have close connections to the sea. Though not as "marine" as the Bajau Laut, the Inuit way of living is closely tied to the marine ecosystem. The hunting of marine mammals, for example, is a key aspect of their tradition. Seals and whales provide the majority of the materials needed to make meals, clothing, tools, and even oil for light. The Inuit also have close ties to the land, hunting terrestrial mammals such as caribou, fox, wolf, muskox, and hare, if found in their region.

The Quechua of South America are a large group of indigenous people belonging to several smaller traditional societies. They share the common language of Quechua in addition to many other distinct languages. Bolivia, for example, is entirely landlocked, with no coastline. It follows that the Quechua are entirely terrestrial people, surviving by farming and other agricultural practises. They live on a mountainous landscape and exploit the altitude to grow many different crops. They have llamas and other herd animals.

It follows from these three examples that each population occupies a different ecosystem and, therefore, has a different niche. Do the Quechua represent a top-predator? What about the Inuit? What is the relationship that each of these groups have with the ecosystem? Is there a trend in niche differences as we move away from the sea? Has it changed over time? Will it change in the future? Exploring these concepts would take a separate book or even several volumes. But we can gloss over a few examples quickly.

The Arctic is the most rapidly warming place on the planet. It has mostly to do with the relative

An Arctic village.

A Quechua village.

Warming leads to more warming: the dark surfaces of the water and the land are revealed when melting occurs. This further increases warming.

change in the landscape. The ice that covers the sea and land melts with a slight increase in temperature, revealing dark water or land underneath. Dark absorbs more radiation and warms, preventing the accumulation of snow later and later into the season. It is a positive feedback loop; the more melting, the more warming, and the more warming, the more melting. The effect in the Arctic is earlier ice break-up over the sea, and snow melt over the land. The Inuit travel in many ways but travelling over snow and ice is important; they can travel to neighbouring communities that are not connected by roads, they hunt and fish on the ice, and they run dog teams on the snow. Nowadays, the snowmobile has become just as important as the boat.

But imagine living in a community totally adapted to living with snow and ice cover for most of the year, having tools for using on snow and ice, vehicles for snow and ice, housing appropriate to living in snow and ice, and every year there is less snow and there is less ice. What do you do to adapt?

Many studies are being conducted on other Arctic organisms to try to figure out how and if they are adapting. Humans are different in this sense as well because of our complex culture and technology. And cultures and methods of adapting from all over the world are working their way into other cultures.

We will switch now to an example of an Arctic marine mammal because there is a lot more research available on non-human species. Try to imagine how this story might apply to humans and other species, all over the world, from all ecosystems.

Polar bears probably evolved a couple of million years ago from an isolated population of brown bears (the grizzly bear). Grizzly bears occupied the region just south of the Arctic and it is thought that a small population evolved to be able to exploit the niche of "top Arctic predator," which had a vacancy. Imagine a population of grizzly bears in which some of the individuals that had mutations to make them lighter in

The polar bear evolved from a population of brown bears (grizzly bears). They are still able to interbreed.

colour, fatter, or with thicker fur. With a vacant niche and so much food lying out of the ice in the form of delicious seal, natural selection might favour those grizzly bears that could tap into those resources.

The polar bear is a magnificent beast that has undergone relatively "rapid" change. Its white (actually yellowish) fur keeps it well hidden from unsuspecting prey as it blends into the ice. Its external ear flaps are tiny to minimize heat loss. Its head is elongated and narrow to help warm the air that is breathed in through the nose and to allow the bear to stick its face into seal breathing holes when hunting. It is able to reduce its metabolism when food resources are low to conserve energy. It is larger than brown bears in order to conserve heat. These are all hypotheses about why a polar bear looks like a polar bear.

To survive in the Arctic ecosystem, a major niche change was required during the evolution of the polar bear. Northern populations of brown bears, like the grizzly, feed primarily on vegetation and only supplement their diets with protein such as fish or scavenged meat. Polar bears are exclusively carnivorous, feeding primarily on the fat of ringed and bearded seals. The only time that polar bears can effectively hunt seals is when they are lying on the ice. Seals come up on ice in order to give birth and to rest and without the ice, seals are not readily available for polar bears. It means that if the ice continues to break up earlier in the spring and form later in the fall, polar bears will have less access to energy-rich food. It means that either they will have to reduce their energy requirements or seek supplemental energy elsewhere if the species is to survive.

What do you think will happen? Some scientists think that over the next few decades the populations of harbour and harp seals may move northward. So if polar bears could hunt these, perhaps it will be able to meet all of the energy requirements. But those species of seals still require significant ice cover for their breeding season, so the benefit may not last long for the polar bear. It has also been suggested that orcas would be able to take over the niche of the polar bear because it too is a top carnivore but it is not reliant upon

Polar bears rely on hunting seals on the frozen seas. Without the ice, it is nearly impossible to catch a meal.

sea ice to hunt successfully. This would leave the polar bear fit for extinction.

If the melting continues as it has then time will tell us the answer. We can get some idea about what might happen by looking at the more southern populations of polar bears, where melting ice is happening faster than in more northern regions. In Churchill, Manitoba, near the southernmost part of their range, scientists have been studying the polar bears for many years. There it has been observed that the body condition (basically, the amount of fat that a bear carries) has been decreasing, especially in females of breeding age. This has resulted in a lower reproductive effort in females. Able to have up to three cubs per litter, the prevalence of females with only one cub is increasing. Between 1987 and 2004, the polar bear population in the region of Hudson Bay declined by about 20% and the earlier spring ice break-up has been deemed responsible.

Will this happen everywhere that there are polar bears? Not likely. Given that polar bears are spread out around the Arctic, with different environmental, geographical, and biological conditions, we might expect that the response of the polar bear population to climate change would be different depending upon where they are. In Alaska, for example, four polar bears were found deceased in the water, presumably trying to swim to ice-covered water, a distance that was becoming greater to cross. Though it is unlikely that the

Female polar bears are having fewer cubs.

The Atacama desert was once a lush and fertile ecosystem. Now it is the driest non-polar region on Earth.

entire Alaskan population of polar bears will go out to sea and drown, it certainly does suggest that bears in that region have to use more energy to meet their needs, something that will compromise reproduction and the population size overall, but in a different way than in Churchill, Manitoba.

What other changes are possible? Imagine that the population did not just die out, imagine that polar bears, faced with increasing temperatures, were surviving but changing. Imagine that natural selection was allowing those individuals better adapted to living in a changing or warming climate to pass on more of their genetic material. What might we expect? To answer this, we must take into account the natural history of the species. Therefore, the list that follows is not at all transferable to humans, but you can certainly ask yourself what the "human equivalent" might be.

Scientists from around the world have speculated on what might happen to the polar bear. The following is a short list:

1) shifting geographic range;
2) increased adult aggression/cannibalism;
3) change in diet to include more vegetation or terrestrial sources.

If any or all of these things happen, it would represent an important niche change in the polar bear. And, if any of these things happen, those individuals that were better at doing them would be more likely to pass on their genetic information that might allow their offspring to do it better as well.

Let us get back to humans because something similar may have happened to humans somewhere between 100,000 and 60,000 years ago. A change in environmental conditions of some sort may have happened where humans evolved. It is, of course, speculative, but there is some evidence to suggest that at about this time, the Earth's climate was cooling and that this led to a decrease in the human population. Some scientists speculate that the population reached as low as only 10,000 individuals. It is still unclear what happened exactly, but a lower temperature may have also caused a decline in sea level, which may have opened up some land bridges previously unavailable. It is possible that once the climate began to heat up again, humans began to move. Some scientists think that only a handful of individuals started migrating, perhaps only 1,000 while others think that the number was considerably higher at 50,000.

From our more recent history, there is an abundance of evidence to describe our responses to changes in climate. In the Atacama Desert in Chile, the driest non-polar region on Earth, there is evidence of ancient human occupation. Once believed to have been a humid and productive landscape, archaeological sites bear the marks of campsites and human activity between 9,500 and 13,000 years old. But the Atacama Desert has gone hundreds of years without a single drop of rain and the lakes have dried up. The people left in search of more hospitable conditions. The people at the time, and likely over several generations as the conditions slowly changed, were able to change their range. There is evidence of such types of mini-migrations in Germany, India, Central Europe, the North American west coast, and Alaska.

Piecing together all of the evidence to create one migration story is still a work in progress. But as of today, it is thought that humans reached Asia sometime between 60,000 and 80,000 years ago. Some humans wandered further East, reaching regions of Oceania by about 45,000 years ago, while others went West to Europe arriving about 40,000 years ago. And it is thought that only about 15,000 years ago did humans make it into the Americas, reaching the Southern tip of South America perhaps only 12,000 years ago. And it seems as though this migration out of Africa coincides with a period of great human innovation; artifacts of jewellery, the oldest yet, have been found with more refined spears and hunting tools, decorated ostrich eggs and materials brought from great distances suggesting developments in the arts and in trade.

It is at this point that we can no longer talk about humans as being all one "thing." It is this great migration that caused our diversification. The migration happened slowly, over generations, with families moving a few kilometres at a time, settling in one place for several generations and then expanding. The expansions were through corridors of similar conditions that, over time, could be seen as a gentle gradient. With each move, the environmental conditions were slightly different; the tools needed to survive were slightly different, the genes most likely to benefit an individual were also slightly different. Time allows for evolution but the migration caused the selection of genetic traits to be in different directions as human populations wandered East, West, or North out of Africa. And without the remixing of the human genome, the human populations became isolated.

We see the effects in the great diversity that is expressed in humans; we see it in our cultures, our languages, our niches. Along the way of the migration routes lay the artifacts to tell the tale of how those who survived to move on lived their lives. With the earliest part of the migration, there is actually very little evidence, only a few tools found in India that match the technology of tools found in Africa, but as we head south, into Oceania, more tools emerge. Interestingly, the tools themselves seem to regress, becoming less refined, more rough. Those tools that were found resembled Neanderthal tools rather than the high technology of the human species that had been around for over 100,000 years. At first it was not believed and anthropologists concluded that the tools continued towards increasing complexity but were made out of materials that were not robust enough to be well preserved (e.g. bamboo). Fair enough. But anthropologist James F. O'Connell at the University of Utah presents another possible explanation. He suggests that the tools were not sophisticated because they did not have to be; Oceania was not previously occupied by any competing species for the niche occupied by humans. Like the case of the evolving polar bear, there was a vacant niche to fill that did not require modern technology or any other "edge."

But the migration of humans into Europe was a completely different story. Neanderthal, *Homo sapiens neanderthalensis* or *Homo neanderthalensis*, however you like, was already there. The similarity of the two species (or subspecies) suggests that both of them filled a very similar niche in their own ecosystems. Merging the two would not be without change. What could have happened? We can go back to our section on niche to understand the options that our character Peaceful John has when Badass Fish comes along. Try applying them here. What are your options?

The end result is that Neanderthals disappear from Southern Spain by about 35,000 years ago and Europe is full to the brim of humans. These examples demonstrate that reproductive isolation (the separation of humans heading east and then south into Oceania, and those that headed north and then west into Europe) and a difference in environment and ecology can lead to different challenges to survival and an increase in diversity.

Hunter gatherers

For the majority of human history, individuals lived as "early" hunter-gatherers. It is difficult to say much more than this and capture the great diversity in niche that early humans occupied. In many respects, the niche of a human population was defined by their tools; the spear throwing mammoth hunter, the bow-and-arrow bison hunter, or the harpoon-throwing whale hunters. And Frank Marlowe, Professor of Anthropology at Harvard University, points out, when talking about the niche of the late hunter-gatherers of the Holocene living in proximity to societies that had already adopted agricultural practise, that even if the conditions are similar, the response can be quite different. Professor Marlowe argues that by studying the late hunter-gatherer societies of recent history, we can piece together what the early hunter-gatherer societies might have been like, especially if we stick primarily to exploring these societies from an ecological niche perspective; an environmental challenge overcome never goes out of fashion.

Though there is great variation among hunter-gatherer societies and, really, we need to consider each one separately, you can begin to derive some central tendencies by looking at a lot of these societies. Well, there are not a lot. But there are some, about 200. And if we collect some basic information about each of them, and organize them by environmental conditions and geographical gradients, some interesting, if not unsurprising, trends have been found.

If we were to stand on the equator together, 12,000 years ago, and I began walking south and you began walking north, we might notice a few of the same things about the human populations that we passed. We would notice that as we walked towards the pole, you the north, and me the south, the amount of "gathering" drops off and the amount of "hunting" increases. This is because the total amount of vegetation decreases as we head towards the poles. The "gathering" part is vegetation. So without it, calories need to be obtained elsewhere. Similarly, more arid environments support less vegetation. For a tribe of

These are just some of the landscapes in which modern hunter-gatherer societies live. Top: Great Victoria Desert, Australia; Centre: The Andaman Islands, India; Bottom: Yasuni National Park, Ecuador.

Based upon these landscapes, in which one would you predict the people hunting and gathering to have the largest range? Why?

_____
_____
_____
_____
_____

Assignment 12: Effects of wandering

Name: _____   Student Number: _____

Fill in the map:

Begin in Central Eastern Africa and draw the migration routes around the world. Fill in the dates along the way. Which way did you go? Did you leave Africa to the south of the Red Sea? Or to the north? Which way is more likely? Use other sources to add more detail.

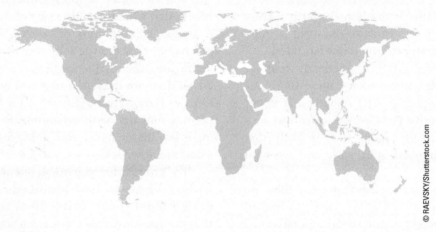

© RAEVSKY/Shutterstock.com

Fill in the table:

Complete the table using two possible responses that a species could exhibit when faced with competition for niche. (Note: there are more than three but just pick your favourite.) Then list the observations that you would have to make in order to support that hypothesis.

Hypothesis: _____	Hypothesis: _____
Observations:	Observations:
1)	1)
2)	2)
3)	3)

Marking:

1) Is the map correct?

2) Is each hypothesis plausible with corresponding observations?

Please see tear out version of Assignment 13 on page 169.

30 hunter-gatherers, it has been estimated that a territory of about 400 square kilometres would be required; a drier "steppe" environment (shrubland) would require a territory of up to 2,000 square kilometres.

Perhaps you are wondering "well, but even in regions of high vegetation, why not hunt anyway?" There are more calories in a piece of meat of the same weight as a tuber, of course. But note that hunting comes at some considerable risk to the personal health of the hunter and it usually requires more energy. In addition, meat is more scarce than vegetation at the lower latitudes.

In later hunter-gatherer societies as we move towards the poles, men become increasingly responsible for acquiring food resources. It is not known when parity between the sexes was lost. Chimpanzees display parity so it is likely that it happened after the split with our common ancestor.

As anadromous fish (fish that spend their life at sea and return to freshwater rivers to spawn) become increasingly important in a population's diet, cultural complexity, including tool making, increases in addition to a more sedentary lifestyle. It is reasonable to think that humans were more mobile before the onset of fishing as an individual's geographic range increases with an increasing reliance upon hunting. Similarly, in very warm climates, where hunter-gatherers gather more and hunt less, home ranges are much smaller.

Today there are only a handful of hunter-gatherer populations that have remained isolated from the modern agricultural world. The people of North Sentinel Island, part of the Andaman Islands archipelago in the Bay of Bengal, have been violently defending their island from any contact. It is thought that the people arrived 60,000 years ago and they are considered to be the most isolated population in the world.

The transition

Perhaps the greatest change to the human species and our relationship with the environment was our switch from hunting and gathering to agriculture as a means of acquiring food and other resources. It did not happen overnight and it did not happen because of a mutation. There is evidence to demonstrate that it took many thousands of years for the first glimmer of crop cultivation to evolve into deliberate acts of agriculture and plant domestication and it happened in several locations around the world at approximately the same time.

To get to agriculture, it appears as if the first step was to engage in forest gardening. The idea here is that a family tends a part of the forest that contains plants that are of value. These are wild plants, but they are specially cared for, and competing and undesirable species are removed. Forest gardens are likely the first and most resilient form of ecosystem modification for human purposes. Compared with agriculture, forest gardening is low maintenance and highly resilient but at a cost and low yield.

To "grow" a forest garden, one needs only to find it. When you have identified a part of the natural forest that contains all of the resources that you need, perhaps fruits, tubers, nuts, and vines, you simply begin to care for these plants. You might cut down some of the forest canopy to allow more light in for your plants, you might pick the weeds surrounding them, and maybe even bring water to them on occasion. But you would not collect seed, select seeds from more desirable plants, clear large areas of land, or plant anything deliberately. You simply rely on what is naturally there and focus your efforts on that area.

The resilience of a system is defined as its ability to overcome a negative pressure. Basically, how well it will recover from disaster. For plants, disasters come in the form of drought, heavy rains, disease, and pests. A forest garden is exceptionally resilient because it exists at different tiers and contains many species with higher genetic variation. Tiers are important for the physical negative pressures. High winds or rains can be defended against by a physical barrier. Forest gardens usually grow at many levels, with high canopy trees, low canopy trees, shrubs, and ground cover. The high canopy trees not only protect from above, but their deep root systems protect the garden against erosion from flooding. High species diversity means that if one species fails, there are still others that might survive to feed you. And high genetic variation among individuals of a single species means that those able to fight off disease or pests may yield food and allow you to survive.

But the trade-off of a forest garden is low yield. Large-scale monocultures (single species crops) can produce staggering amounts of food if they are successful. A forest garden may only contain one or two plants of each species giving greater variety, but much less food (or other resource) of each kind.

The forest garden remains still an important component of traditional life in Central Sulawesi, Indonesia. In the past, before agriculture, it likely represented the source for the majority of a family's resources. Nowadays, the forest garden is considered a "safety net" during hardship though in some regions, the resources of the family forest garden can represent up to 77% of the annual household income. Studies of these forest garden systems reveal the real human impact when compared with natural forests. For example, forest gardens contain 32–40 species per hectare, whereas natural forests contain up to 92 species per hectare. Species reduction is therefore an important component. Perhaps you are wondering why expend energy removing trees and plants that are not useful, why not just let them grow? Within an ecosystem, there is a limited amount of available nutrients and other resources like water and sunlight. You do not want to let the useless plants take away from the useful plants. That is why it is a good idea to remove the weeds from vegetable gardens. The forest gardens contained species that were important economically, including coffee, cocoa, and cassava, species that were favoured by the family, including spices or particular vegetables, and medicinal plants. The further the family lived from access to modern medicine, the more diverse was their collection of medicinal plants in their garden.

Nowadays, forest gardens are also deliberately planted, capitalizing on the great resilience and protection that the framework provides. But originally, as the technology was developing, it is thought that only plants that were there, and of value, were tended. Nothing was brought in. It does not seem like a great leap, however, to imagine that careful plant husbandry may lead to advancement towards planting and domestication.

Using the words "high", "intermediate," and "low," fill in the blanks for each of these images:

Resilience: _____   _____   _____
Maintenance: _____   _____   _____
Yield: _____   _____   _____
Diversity: _____   _____   _____

Agriculture

Most humans currently living are "farmers," in the broadest sense. Most of us survive off of the products of farming. You could say that "farming" is a form of niche. Over the last few thousand years, and particularly in the last hundred or so, we have innovated agriculture to maximize efficiency and yield. When it all started, however, things were quite a bit different.

Although there is evidence of agriculture having evolved independently in several places around the world, most of the archaeological evidence comes from what is commonly known as the Fertile Crescent, namely Iraq, Kuwait, Syria, Lebanon, Jordan, Israel, Palestine, Cyprus, and Egypt. In this region there was a culture of humans that "transitioned" from hunting and gathering to farming

Now a dry and scraggly landscape, this region was lush and fertile 15,000 years ago.

A reconstructed Neolithic dugout home in Jordan.

over a period of a couple of thousand years. They were the Natufians.

The appearance of the Natufian culture occurred about 13,000 years ago. With over 60 known archaeological sites, the evidence is plentiful, spread throughout the Fertile Crescent and in great abundance. It is an archaeologist's dream and of no surprise that the Natufians are some of the best studied ancient people. The early Natufians lived in semi-permanent settlements made of partially dugout huts with a stone foundation and walls likely made from reeds or twigs. There is very little evidence of storage facilities, suggesting that what was gathered and hunted was consumed readily. A few observations about the burial practises of the Natufians have compelling cultural interpretations. About 30% of the buried bones found are of children. Archaeologists believe that this is indicative of increasing social stressors as population densities increased. Also, a close association of canine and human bones in two grave areas has been interpreted as a sign that the gap between "human" and the "natural world" was on the decline. There is also great variability in burial practise among the different populations, and recent evidence suggests that there was likely no special treatment of people of higher social class.

The tools found associated with the early Natufians are those of hunter-gatherers. Sickles were invented to maximize yield from wild cereals, and food-processing tools such as mortars and pestles were used to grind wild vegetation. The few seeds that have been found have all been deemed to be wild gatherings. The bones of many edible mammals have been found, including cattle, gazelle, ibex, hare, and sheep. Fish, though not a staple, were certainly accessed, especially in populations in the north of their range.

The climatic phenomenon known as the Younger Dryas (14,000–12,000 years ago) was a major environmental paradigm shift that affected the entire ecosystem. The climate cooled and dried, changing the landscape dramatically. The wild cereals and grains would have suffered, resulting in a decline in their populations and increased competition among Natufians and other gathering societies would have taxed what little remained. The response was variable; some populations became more mobile, returning to their native settlements to bury their dead, while others began to deliberately plant wild seeds and tend to them. Or so it was/is thought. There is no doubt that the Natufian culture lived during the time of the Younger Dryas and that they survived through this dramatic climate change. But recently, the evidence suggesting that they domesticated wild plant species and deliberately grew them has been questioned.

It goes back and forth. The cooling and drying of the climate would have reduced the cereal and grain species. But there is evidence to suggest that the wild gazelle population increased during that time. This is an observation that is inconsistent with declining plant resources. There is also evidence that the consumption of freshwater fish increased and this is inconsistent with a drought hypothesis. And even though the Natufians are firmly associated with the transition to agriculture, the foundation of the argument comes down to nine fat seeds. At Abu Hureyra, in modern Syria, the archaeological site contains artifacts spanning 4,000 years. It was excavated during 1972 and 1973, and during the analysis of the various layers, nine plump rye seeds were found.

One thousand years passed between the times that people began cultivating crops and evidence of domestication. Domestication requires a change in the genetics of a population through artificial selection. People growing wild cereals would select the fattest or the hardiest or the ones with the thinnest husks and plant them, generation after generation, until all that grew were fat, hardy, and thin husked cereals. Because these desirable traits are selected for and those without those traits are not permitted to reproduce, change can happen very quickly. It is thought that because the weight of a kernel of rye or barley, for example, is controlled by several genes in the DNA, selection for the heaviest is possible but would likely have taken longer to achieve.

What has been established is that the conditions in that area were fluctuating quite a lot. Between 11,00 and 9,000 years ago, after the Younger Dryas, there was a wet period. This was the wettest period in the Holocene thus far and would have resulted in fertile arable lands fit for cultivation. But by 7,000 years ago things were drying up again. In some regions of the Fertile Crescent, irrigation methods evolved in order to overcome the changing climate. In other regions, human populations continued to rely upon natural rain.

On the other side of the argument, permanent settlements of up to 10 times the size of early Natufian settlements arose shortly after the end of the Younger Dryas. How could they have supported such a large population without having already developed agricultural practises during the dryer times? There are also signs of increasing densities of weed species typically associated with cultivated crops. And finally, playing on the idea of a particularly slow progression to official domestication, the suggestion that the Natufians were cultivating wild crops and this would not be recognizable as agricultural activity to archeobotanists.

Irrespective of when, precisely, and by whom exactly, agriculture evolved, its impact on the natural world is without precedent. Extended periods of agricultural activity on the same land causes nutrient depletion, soil instability, and changes in the natural water table. We have fundamentally altered our natural world in ways that many scientists believe will not be easily undone.

From wild to domestic

Agricultural activity had the effect of domesticating previously wild species. Imagine a scenario in which you collect wild pea pods and plant them in a garden. Then, once those plants have sprouted, you select the largest pea pods and, instead of eating them, you plant those. And then from the second generation, you plant only the largest pods, etc... Over time, the genetic make-up of your pea plants would have far more "large pea pod" genes than "small pea pod" genes. Over a bit more time, you may have only plants with large pea pods. This is the story of the majority of our food. From vegetables to our family pets, the vast majority of

Domesticated (left) and wild (right) strawberries.

the species with which we interact are domesticated. But domestication is not just about finding yourself in an ecosystem that includes humans. It is about not being yourself at all.

To understand the significance of domestication, we need to consider two other conditions: wild and tame. A wild species is one where there has not been any alteration in either the genotype, or the phenotype due to artificial selection by humans (we can debate the necessity of the word "human" to be included in the definition). It means that the species' genetic code has not been tampered with, and that reproduction among individuals is determined by natural processes, uninfluenced by humans. In addition to maintaining the wild genotype, the species also maintains a wild phenotype. It means that their phenotype (remember, phenotype is determined by both the genes and the environment) has not been affected by humans in any way.

The aurochs of Europe, now extinct, was a wild cow. A colder climate 5 million years ago caused the opening up of thick forest and the expansion of grasslands. What followed was the evolution of several large grazing species, including the auroch. The species likely evolved in modern-day India and migrated towards Europe, arriving 270,000 years ago. Now preserved in ancient cave paintings, it is clear that the aurochs was valued by *Homo sapiens sapiens* as a source of meat, leather, and bone. It is thought that the aurochs was domesticated independently two times, one in India, and the other in the Near East, about 9,000 years ago. The Indian domestication resulted in a humped cow. Likely a grassland grazer, the aurochs lived in small herds of approximately 50 individuals. They were fierce tempered and

The aurochs.

> ### Look it up . . .
>
> Can you find an example where a species other than humans is responsible for domesticating another species?
>
> _____
>
> _____
>
> _____

were said to fight off packs of hungry wolves. The last one died in Poland in 1627. Yet, the domesticated descendents remain and have proliferated with about 800 distinct breeds found worldwide.

There is a distinct and important intermediate stage between wild and domesticated. Tame individuals retain their original wild genotype but they have an altered phenotype. The alteration is, usually, the ability to live in close proximity to humans. If you remember from earlier on, the phenotype is determined by both the genetic composition and the environment. In the case of tameness, the environment is "humans." In fact, not only must the wild population be in contact with humans, the humans have to exert "ownership" over them. This limits the number of species available for domestication events because in order to be owned, the species must be able to survive in a variety of climates, be gregarious, be able to breed in captive conditions, and not frighten easily.

One observation made by archaeologists studying the process of domestication is that when a species is at the very early stage of domestication, it is structurally smaller. You might expect that humans at the time would be selecting for the largest animals. But actually, this trend towards a reduction in size has been observed all over. Why would you find that early domestication led to a reduction in the size of the individuals? Perhaps you can think of several hypotheses. Is it possible that they were being selected for their calm temperament and that larger animals were often more aggressive? Could it be that they were unable to provide the equivalent of the natural diet and so individuals did not grow as large as if in the wild? Could it be that the larger ones were eaten before they could be bred? The size of the brain is also reduced and the reason for this is rather unclear.

Along with smaller size goes a tendency towards neoteny. That is, a tendency to appear more juvenile. The reason for this is even more unclear in those species that were not being selected for their "cuteness." But even so, domesticated species appear more like the juvenile of the wild species than the adult. And some anthropologists might

The Belgian blue bull.

© Eric Isselee/Shutterstock.com

even point out that the same could be said of the species *Homo sapiens sapiens*.

The Belgian blue bull is a massive beast. Its muscular body is not the result of hormones such as steroids, but rather a mutation in the DNA that causes muscle fibres to double up and reduce the amount of fat accumulation. They also have less bone. First documented in 1807, this mutation has been selected and bred to the point of being "fixed" within the Belgian blue and the Piedmontese breeds of domestic cattle. Pregnant cows often require a caesarean section to deliver their calves because the doubling up of muscle mass occurs during early development. But the

---

Think about it . . .

Why can a species that has been domesticated by selective breeding be considered a GMO?

_____

_____

_____

_____

Why is a domesticated species created by selective breeding different than today's GMOs?

_____

_____

_____

_____

benefit to humans is that there is more meat, especially of the choice cuts.

Therefore, domesticated species, all of them, might be considered genetically modified. This is because breeders are identifying the mutations that naturally occur in the population of the species that they are cultivating or farming and then making sure to breed those individuals to eventually change the genetic make-up of the entire crop or herd. But today's definition of genetically modified organism (GMO) includes the requirement of using genetic engineering techniques such as causing a mutation or inserting or deleting a gene. So, technically, all domesticated species would not therefore be considered GMOs. However, selective breeding is a precursor that often gives a similar result: a favourable difference in phenotype that is useful to humans. It just takes a lot longer and you have no control over which variation appears in the initial population.

Final thoughts

This is not the end. We have simply just run out of time. Writing the last chapter of this book was a real challenge for us. As humans began to diversify, figuring out which were the common themes to include became difficult and frustrating, and then we thought that it would be best to leave these topics to our discussions in class and to keep track of them for subsequent editions of the book!

So this is a work in progress. We still have to tell you about what happens after domestication. But, actually, most of the niche changes and the big paradigm shifts have already been described. What comes after that is just, well, upgrades.

Create your own timeline here:

13.8 Billion

4.5 Billion

3.8 Billion

3.4 Billion

1.8 Billion

1.0 Billion

550 Million

530 Million

400 Million

395 Million

320 Million

235 Million

68 Million

66 Million

60 Million

47 Million

15–20 Million

11.9 Million

6 Million

3.7 Million

3.4 Million

2.6–1.7 Million

1.9 Million

0.5 Million

0.2 Million

0.195 Million

0.07 Million

0.01 Million

Bibliography

Agosta, W. C. (1997). Medicines and Drugs from Plants. *Journal of Chemical Education, 74*(7), 857–860.

Aiello, L. C., & Wheeler, P. (2009). Wenner-Gren Foundation for Anthropological Research Evolution. *Current Anthropology, 36*(2), 199–221.

Albert, R. M., Berna, F., & Goldberg, P. (2012). Insights on Neanderthal fire use at Kebara Cave (Israel) through high resolution study of prehistoric combustion features: Evidence from phytoliths and thin sections. *Quaternary International, 247*(1), 278–293. http://doi.org/10.1016/j.quaint.2010.10.016

Ambrose, S. H. (2001). Paleolithic technology and human evolution. *Science (New York, N.Y.), 291*(5509), 1748–1753. http://doi.org/10.1126/science.1059487

Anonymous. (2002). *Report from the ICSU Study Group on Science and Traditional Knowledge.*

Anonymous. (2011a). *Protecting India ' s Traditional Knowledge.*

Anonymous. (2011b). Women have stronger immune systems than men and it's all down to Xchromosome related microRNA. Retrieved from www.sciencedaily.com/releases/2011/09/110927192352.htm

Anonymous. (2014). Single celled Algae Took The Leap To Multicellularity 200 Million Years Ago. Retrieved from http://www.sciencedaily.com/releases/2009/02/090219140546.htm

Arsuaga, J. L., Martínez, I., Arnold, L. J., Aranburu, a, Gracia-Téllez, a, Sharp, W. D., . . . Carbonell, E. (2014). Neandertal roots: Cranial and chronological evidence from Sima de los Huesos. *Science (New York, N.Y.), 344*(6190), 1358–63. http://doi.org/10.1126/science.1253958

Audi, R. (2009). The Sources of Knowledge. *Oxford Handbooks Online*, (September), 1–15. http://doi.org/10.1093/oxfordhb/9780195301700.003.0003

Bada, J., & Lazcano, A. (2000). Stanley Miller's 70th birthday. *Origins of Life and Evolution of Biosphere, 30*, 107–112. http://doi.org/10.1023/A:1006746205180

Balter, M. (2001). In search of the first Europeans. *Science (New York, N.Y.), 291*(5509), 1722–1725. http://doi.org/10.1126/science.291.5509.1722

Balter, M. (2010). Archaeology. The tangled roots of agriculture. *Science (New York, N.Y.), 327*(5964), 404–406. http://doi.org/10.1126/science.327.5964.404

Bar-Yosef, O. (1998). The Natufian Culture in the Levant. *Evolutionary Anthropology, 6*(5), 159–177. http://doi.org/10.2307/530343

Bekker, a, Holland, H. D., Wang, P.-L., Rumble, D., Stein, H. J., Hannah, J. L., . . . Beukes, N. J. (2004). Dating the rise of atmospheric oxygen. *Nature, 427*(6970), 117–120. http://doi.org/10.1038/nature02260

Bogaard, A. (2005). "Garden agriculture" and the nature of early farming in Europe and the Near East. *World Archaeology, 37*(2), 177–196. http://doi.org/10.1080/00438240500094572

Bouali, H.-E., Zgal, M., & Ben Lakhdar, Z. (2005). Popularisation of Optical Phenomena: Establishing the First Ibn Al-Haytham Workshop on Photography. *ETOP, ETOP080,* 327–330.

Brainard, M. S., & Doupe, A. J. (2002). What songbirds teach us about learning. *Nature, 417*(6886), 351–358. http://doi.org/10.1038/417351a

Buckley, L. (2007). This chimp is made for walking. *News@ Nature*, (July 2007), 1–2. http://doi.org/10.1038/news070716-2

Burne, J. (2002). Animal instinct. *The Guardian*, (January 17).

Calnek, E. E., Edward, P., Paul, C., & Macneish, R. S. (2009). Settlement Pattern and Chinampa Agriculture at Tenochtitlan. *American Antiquity, 37*(1), 104–115.

Cardinale, B. J., Duffy, J. E., Gonzalez, A., Hooper, D. U., Perrings, C., Venail, P., . . . Naeem, S. (2012). Corrigendum: Biodiversity loss and its impact on humanity. *Nature, 489*(7415), 326–326. http://doi.org/10.1038/nature11373

Carrier, D. R. (2011). The advantage of standing up to fight and the evolution of habitual bipedalism in hominins. *PLoS ONE, 6*(5), e19630. http://doi.org/10.1371/journal.pone.0019630

Casanovas-Vilar, I., Alba, D. M., Moyà-Solà, S., Galindo, J., Cabrera, L., Garcés, M., . . . Angelone, C. (2008). Biochronological, taphonomical, and paleoenvironmental background of the fossil great ape Pierolapithecus catalaunicus (Primates, Hominidae). *Journal of Human Evolution, 55*(4), 589–603. http://doi.org/10.1016/j.jhevol.2008.05.004

Chamberlain, E. B. (1916). Shorter Notes. *The Bryologist, 19*(6), 95. http://doi.org/10.1639/0007-2745(1916)19[95:SN]2.0.CO;2

Chimpanzee, T. T., Diamond, J., & Three, C. (2009). Five Questions on Human Sexuality.

Cooper, R. (2015). Why Do We Have Wisdom Teeth ? asks Rachele Cooper, a scienceline staff member. Retrieved from http://scienceline.org/2007/02/askcooperwisdomteeth/

Descamps-julien, A. B., & Gonzalez, A. (2014). Stable Coexistence in a Fluctuating Environment : An Experimental Demonstration Stable Coexistence in A Fluctuating Environment: An Experimental Demonstration. *Ecology*, *86*(10), 2815–2824.

Dettwyler, K. a. (2004). When to wean: biological versus cultural perspectives. *Clinical Obstetrics and Gynecology*, *47*(3), 712–723. http://doi.org/10.1097/01.grf.0000137217.97573.01

Egerton, F. N. (1968). Leeuwenhoek as a founder of animal demography. *Journal of the History of Biology*, *1*(1), 1–22. http://doi.org/10.1007/BF00149773

Elekta. (1993). *Intelligent design. Brenner's Encyclopedia of Genetics, Second Edition* (Vol. 72). Elsevier Inc. http://doi.org/10.1049/me:19930053

Emmett Duffy, J. (2009). Why biodiversity is important to the functioning of real-world ecosystems. *Frontiers in Ecology and the Environment*, *7*(8), 437–444. http://doi.org/10.1890/070195

Falk, D. (1990). Brain evolution in Homo: The "radiator" theory. *Behavioral and Brain Sciences*, *13*(02), 333–344. http://doi.org/10.1017/S0140525X00078973

Falk, D., Redmond, J. C., Guyer, J., Conroy, C., Recheis, W., Weber, G. W., & Seidler, H. (2000). Early hominid brain evolution: a new look at old endocasts. *Journal of Human Evolution*, *38*(5), 695–717. http://doi.org/10.1006/jhev.1999.0378

Fargione, J., Brown, C. S., & Tilman, D. (2003). Community assembly and invasion: an experimental test of neutral versus niche processes. *Proceedings of the National Academy of Sciences of the United States of America*, *100*(15), 8916–8920. http://doi.org/10.1073/pnas.1033107100

Feldman, R. P., & Goodrich, J. T. (1999). The Edwin Smith Surgical Papyrus. *Child's Nerv Syst*, *15*, 281–284.

Fonseca-Azevedo, K., & Herculano-Houzel, S. (2012). Metabolic constraint imposes tradeoff between body size and number of brain neurons in human evolution. *Proceedings of the National Academy of Sciences*, *109*(8), 1–6. http://doi.org/10.1073/pnas.1206390109

Frey, S. H. (2008). Tool use, communicative gesture and cerebral asymmetries in the modern human brain. *Philosophical Transactions of the Royal Society of London. Series B, Biological Sciences*, *363*(1499), 1951–1957. http://doi.org/10.1098/rstb.2008.0008

Germonpré, M., Sablin, M. V., Stevens, R. E., Hedges, R. E. M., Hofreiter, M., Stiller, M., & Després, V. R. (2009). Fossil dogs and wolves from Palaeolithic sites in Belgium, the Ukraine and Russia: osteometry, ancient DNA and stable isotopes. *Journal of Archaeological Science*, *36*(2), 473–490. http://doi.org/10.1016/j.jas.2008.09.033

Germonpré, M., Udrescu, M., & Fiers, E. (2014). Possible evidence of mammoth hunting at the Neanderthal site of Spy (Belgium). *Quaternary International*, *337*, 28–42. http://doi.org/10.1016/j.quaint.2012.10.035

Gibbons, A. (2014). Neandertals and Moderns Made Imperfect Mates. *Science*, *343*(6170), 471–472. http://doi.org/10.1126/science.343.6170.471

Gingerich, P. D. (1990). African dawn for primates. *Palaeontographica*, *214*, 31–56.

Gravel, D., & Principle, C. E. (2014). Assembly Models. Retrieved from http://www.oxfordbibliographies.com/view/document/obo-978

Green, R. E., Krause, J., Briggs, A. W., Maricic, T., Stenzel, U., Kircher, M., . . . Pääbo, S. (2010). A draft sequence of the Neandertal genome. *Science (New York, N.Y.)*, *328*(5979), 710–722. http://doi.org/10.1126/science.1188021

Grime, J. (2002). Declining plant diversity : empty niches or functional shifts ? *Journal of Vegetation Science*, *13*(4), 457–460. http://doi.org/10.1658/1100-9233(2002)013[0457:DPDENO]2.0.CO;2

Grosberg, R. K., & Strathmann, R. R. (2007). The Evolution of Multicellularity: A Minor Major Transition? *Annual Review of Ecology, Evolution, and Systematics*, *38*(1), 621–654. http://doi.org/10.1146/annurev.ecolsys.36.102403.114735

Guelpa, P. (2015). Study finds mammals diversified only after the extinction of dinosaurs. Retrieved from http://www.wsws.org/en/articles/2013/02/22/mammf22.html?view=print

Gupta, A. K. (2004). Origin of agriculture and domestication of plants and animals linked to early Holocene climate amelioration. *Current Science*, *87*(1), 54–59. http://doi.org/10.1111/j.1365-2443.2008.01212.x

Gupta, R., Gabrielsen, B., & Ferguson, S. M. (2005). Nature's medicines: traditional knowledge and intellectual property management. *Curr Drug Discov Technol*, *2*(4), 203–219.

Guynup, S. (n.d.). The mating game : ligers , zorses , wholphins , and other hybrid animals raise a beastly science question : what is a species?

Hammond, A. S., Alba, D. M., Almécija, S., & Moyà-Solà, S. (2013). Middle Miocene Pierolapithecus provides a first glimpse into early hominid pelvic morphology. *Journal of Human Evolution*, *64*(6), 658–666. http://doi.org/10.1016/j.jhevol.2013.03.002

Hammond, A. S., & Ward, C. V. (2013). Australopithecus and Kenyanthropus. In *A Companion to Paleoanthropology* (pp. 434–456). Blackwell Publishing Ltd. http://doi.org/10.1002/9781118332344.ch23

Hamon, C. (2008). Functional analysis of stone grinding and polishing tools from the earliest Neolithic of northwestern Europe. *Journal of Archaeological Science*, *35*(6), 1502–1520. http://doi.org/10.1016/j.jas.2007.10.017

Hamrick, M. W., Churchill, S. E., Schmitt, D., & Hylander, W. L. (1998). EMG of the human flexor pollicis longus muscle: implications for the evolution of hominid tool use. *Journal of Human Evolution*, *34*(2), 123–136. http://doi.org/10.1006/jhev.1997.0177

Hardy, K., Buckley, S., Collins, M. J., Estalrrich, A., Broth-well, D., Copeland, L., . . . Rosas, A. (2012). Neanderthal medics? Evidence for food, cooking, and medicinal plants entrapped in dental calculus. *Naturwissenschaften*, *99*(8), 617–626. http://doi.org/10.1007/s00114-012-0942-0

Harpole, W. S., & Tilman, D. (2007). Grassland species loss resulting from reduced niche dimension. *Nature*, *446*(7137), 791–793. http://doi.org/10.1038/nature05684

Hartwig-Scherer, S. (1991). Was "Lucy" more human than her "child"? Observations on early hominid postcranial skeletons. *Journal of Human Evolution*, *21*(6), 439–449. http://doi.org/10.1016/0047-2484(91)90094-C

Harvati-Papatheodorou, K. (2013). Neanderthals. In *A Companion to Paleoanthropology*. Blackwell Publishing Ltd.

Health, T., Earth, P., Strange, S., Animals, N., Human, H., Shop, N., . . . Origins, H. (2015). Earliest Great Ape Had Posture Like Humans ,. Retrieved from http://www.livescience.com/29277oldestgreatapehadhumanposture.html

Holt, R. D. (2009). IJEE Soapbox: Prince Kropotkin meets the Hutchinsonian niche. *Israel Journal of Ecology and Evolution*, *55*(1), 1–10. http://doi.org/10.1560/IJEE.55.1.1

Hu, Y., Meng, J., Wang, Y., & Li, C. (2005). Large Mesozoic mammals fed on young dinosaurs. *Nature*, *433*(7022), 149–152. http://doi.org/10.1038/nature03102

Hubbe, M., Hanihara, T., & Harvati, K. (2009). Climate signatures in the morphological differentiation of worldwide modern human populations. *Anatomical Record*, *292*(11), 1720–1733. http://doi.org/10.1002/ar.20976

Hutchinson, G. . E. . (1959). Homage to Santa Rosalia or Why are there so many kinds of animals? *The American Naturalist*, *93*(870), 145–159.

Hutchinson, G. . E. . (1961a). Paradox of Plankton.Pdf. *American Naturalist*, *95*(882), 137–145.

Hutchinson, G. . E. . (1961b). The Paradox of the Plankton Author. *The American Naturalist*, *95*(882), 137–145. http://doi.org/10.1086/282171

Ingalhalikar, M., Smith, A., Parker, D., Satterthwaite, T. D., Elliott, M. a, Ruparel, K., . . . Verma, R. (2014). Sex differences in the structural connectome of the human brain. *Proceedings of the National Academy of Sciences of the United States of America*, *111*(2), 823–8. http://doi.org/10.1073/pnas.1316909110

Iriki, a., & Taoka, M. (2012). Triadic (ecological, neural, cognitive) niche construction: a scenario of human brain evolution extrapolating tool use and language from the control of reaching actions. *Philosophical Transactions of the Royal Society B: Biological Sciences*, *367*(1585), 10–23. http://doi.org/10.1098/rstb.2011.0190

Jelinek, J. (1969). Neanderthal Man and Homo sapiens in Central and Eastern Europe. *Current Anthropology*, *10*(5), 475. http://doi.org/10.1086/201049

John, B., & Wilford, N. (2015). Fossils Found in Spain Seen as Last Link to Great Apes. *New York Times*, pp. 11–13.

Kennedy, M. J., & Droser, M. L. (2011). Early Cambrian metazoans in fluvial environments, evidence of the non-marine Cambrian radiation. *Geology*, *39*(6), 583–586. http://doi.org/10.1130/G32002.1

Key, A. J. M., & Lycett, S. J. (2011). Technology based evolution? A biometric test of the effects of hand-size versus tool form on efficiency in an experimental cutting task. *Journal of Archaeological Science*, *38*(7), 1663–1670. http://doi.org/10.1016/j.jas.2011.02.032

Koser, K. (2010). *Introduction: International migration and global governance. Global Governance* (Vol. 16). http://doi.org/10.1093/acprof

Krause, J., Lalueza-Fox, C., Orlando, L., Enard, W., Green, R. E., Burbano, H. a., . . . Pääbo, S. (2007). The Derived FOXP2 Variant of Modern Humans Was Shared with Neandertals. *Current Biology*, *17*(21), 1908–1912. http://doi.org/10.1016/j.cub.2007.10.008

Kuipers, R. S., Luxwolda, M. F., Dijck-Brouwer, D. a J., Eaton, S. B., Crawford, M. a, Cordain, L., & Muskiet, F. a J. (2010). Estimated macronutrient and fatty acid intakes from an East African Paleolithic diet. *The British Journal of Nutrition*, *104*(11), 1666–1687. http://doi.org/10.1017/S0007114510002679

Kylafis, G., & Loreau, M. (2011). Niche construction in the light of niche theory. *Ecology Letters*, *14*(2), 82–90. http://doi.org/10.1111/j.1461-0248.2010.01551.x

Lai, C. S. L., Gerrelli, D., Monaco, A. P., Fisher, S. E., & Copp, A. J. (2003). FOXP2 expression during brain development coincides with adult sites of pathology in a severe speech and language disorder. *Brain*, *126*(11), 2455–2462. http://doi.org/10.1093/brain/awg247

Leonard, J. a, Wayne, R. K., Wheeler, J., Valadez, R., Guillén, S., & Vilà, C. (2002). Ancient DNA evidence for Old World origin of New World dogs. *Science (New York, N.Y.)*, *298*(5598), 1613–1616. http://doi.org/10.1126/science.1076980

Levine, J. M., & HilleRisLambers, J. (2009). The importance of niches for the maintenance of species diversity. *Nature*, *461*(7261), 254–257. http://doi.org/10.1038/nature08251

Lewis, D. a, Kamon, E., & Hodgson, J. L. (1986). Physiological differences between genders. Implications for sports conditioning. *Sports Medicine (Auckland, N.Z.)*, *3*(5), 357–369. http://doi.org/10.2165/00007256-198603050-00005

Lovejoy, C. O., Suwa, G., Spurlock, L., Asfaw, B., & White, T. D. (2009). The pelvis and femur of Ardipithecus ramidus: the emergence of upright walking. *Science (New York, N.Y.)*, *326*(5949), 71e1–e6. http://doi.org/10.1126/science.1175831

MacArthur, R. H. (2011). Population Ecology of Some Warblers of Northeastern Coniferous Forests. *Ecology*, *39*(4), 599–619.

MacDougall, A. S., Gilbert, B., & Levine, J. M. (2009). Plant invasions and the niche. *Journal of Ecology*, *97*(4), 609–615. http://doi.org/10.1111/j.1365-2745.2009.01514.x

Marcus, G. F., & Fisher, S. E. (2003). FOXP2 in focus: What can genes tell us about speech and language? *Trends in Cognitive Sciences*, *7*(6), 257–262. http://doi.org/10.1016/S1364-6613(03)00104-9

Maricic, T., Günther, V., Georgiev, O., Gehre, S., Ćurlin, M., Schreiweis, C., . . . Pääbo, S. (2013). A recent evolutionary change affects a regulatory element in the human FOXP2 gene. *Molecular Biology and Evolution*, *30*(4), 844–852. http://doi.org/10.1093/molbev/mss271

Martin, R. a, & Pfennig, D. W. (2012). Widespread disruptive selection in the wild is associated with intense resource competition. *BMC Evolutionary Biology*, *12*(1), 136. http://doi.org/10.1186/1471-2148-12-136

Mason, P. H., & Short, R. V. (2011). Neanderthal-human hybrids. *Hypothesis*, *9*(1), 1–5. http://doi.org/10.5779/hypothesis.v9i1.215

Matsuoka, Y., Vigouroux, Y., Goodman, M. M., Sanchez G, J., Buckler, E., & Doebley, J. (2002). A single domestication for maize shown by multilocus microsatellite genotyping. *Proceedings of the National Academy of Sciences of the United States of America*, *99*(9), 6080–6084. http://doi.org/10.1073/pnas.052125199

Matthews, B., De Meester, L., Jones, C. G., Ibelings, B. W., Bouma, T. J., Nuutinen, V., . . . Odling-Smee, J. (2014). Under niche construction: An operational bridge between ecology, evolution, and ecosystem science. *Ecological Monographs*, *84*(2), 245–263. http://doi.org/10.1890/13-0953.1

McPeek, M. a. (2014). Limiting Factors, Competitive Exclusion, and a More Expansive View of Species Coexistence. *The American Naturalist*, *183*(3), iii–iv. http://doi.org/10.1086/675305

McPherron, S. P., Alemseged, Z., Marean, C. W., Wynn, J. G., Reed, D., Geraads, D., . . . Béarat, H. a. (2010). Evidence for stone-tool-assisted consumption of animal tissues before 3.39 million years ago at Dikika, Ethiopia. *Nature*, *466*(7308), 857–860. http://doi.org/10.1038/nature09248

Meredith, R. W., Janečka, J. E., Gatesy, J., Ryder, O. a, Fisher, C. a, Teeling, E. C., . . . Murphy, W. J. (2011). Impacts of the Cretaceous Terrestrial Revolution and KPg extinction on mammal diversification. *Science (New York, N.Y.)*, *334*(6055), 521–4. http://doi.org/10.1126/science.1211028

Merrill, W. L., Hard, R. J., Mabry, J. B., Fritz, G. J., Adams, K. R., Roney, J. R., & MacWilliams, a C. (2009). The diffusion of maize to the southwestern United States and its impact. *Proceedings of the National Academy of Sciences of the United States of America*, *106*(50), 21019–21026. http://doi.org/10.1073/pnas.0906075106

Meyer, M., Kircher, M., Gansauge, M.-T., Li, H., Racimo, F., Mallick, S., . . . Paabo, S. (2012). A High-Coverage Genome Sequence from an Archaic Denisovan Individual. *Science*, *338*(6104), 222–226. http://doi.org/10.1126/science.1224344

Miller bio. (n.d.).

Miller, S. L. (1953). A production of amino acids under possible primitive earth conditions. *Science (New York, N.Y.)*. http://doi.org/10.1126/science.117.3046.528

Mir, C., Zerjal, T., Combes, V., Dumas, F., Madur, D., Bedoya, C., . . . Charcosset, a. (2013). Out of America: Tracing the genetic footprints of the global diffusion of maize. *Theoretical and Applied Genetics*, *126*(11), 2671–2682. http://doi.org/10.1007/s00122-013-2164-z

Morris, C. (2009). Milestones in Ecology. *The Princeton Guide to Ecology*, 761–773.

Moya-Sola, S., Kohler, M., Alba, D. M., Casanovas-Vilar, I., & Galindo, J. (2004). Pierolapithecus catalaunicus, a New Middle Miocene Great Ape from Spain, *303*(March), 1831–1838.

Naeem, S., Duffy, J. E., & Zavaleta, E. (2012). The Functions of Biological Diversity in an Age of Extinction. *Science*, *336*(6087), 1401–1406. http://doi.org/10.1126/science.1215855

Nelson, E., Rolian, C., Cashmore, L., & Shultz, S. (2011). Digit ratios predict polygyny in early apes, Ardipithecus, Neanderthals and early modern humans but not in Australopithecus. *Proceedings. Biological Sciences / The Royal Society*, *278*(1711), 1556–1563. http://doi.org/10.1098/rspb.2010.1740

Niedźwiedzki, G., Szrek, P., Narkiewicz, K., Narkiewicz, M., & Ahlberg, P. E. (2010). Tetrapod trackways from the early Middle Devonian period of Poland. *Nature*, *463*(7277), 43–48. http://doi.org/10.1038/nature08623

Nudel, R., & Newbury, D. F. (2013). Foxp2. *Wiley Interdisciplinary Reviews: Cognitive Science*, *4*(5), 547–560. http://doi.org/10.1002/wcs.1247

Overmann, K. a., & Coolidge, F. L. (2013). Human species and mating systems: Neandertal-Homo sapiens reproductive isolation and the archaeological and fossil records. *Journal of Anthropological Sciences*, *91*, 91–110. http://doi.org/10.4436/JASS.91021

Page, J. E., Huffman, M. A., Smith, V., & Towers, G. H. N. (1997). Chemical Basis for Aspilia Leaf-Swallowing by Chimpanzees: A Reanalysis. *Journal of Chemical Ecology*, *23*(9), 2211–2226.

Pang, J. F., Kluetsch, C., Zou, X. J., Zhang, A. B., Luo, L. Y., Angleby, H., . . . Savolainen, P. (2009). MtDNA data indicate a single origin for dogs south of yangtze river, less than 16,300 years ago, from numerous wolves.

Molecular Biology and Evolution, 26(12), 2849–2864. http://doi.org/10.1093/molbev/msp195

Piperno, D. R., Ranere, A. J., Holst, I., Iriarte, J., & Dickau, R. (2009). Starch grain and phytolith evidence for early ninth millennium B.P. maize from the Central Balsas River Valley, Mexico. *Proceedings of the National Academy of Sciences of the United States of America, 106*(13), 5019–5024. http://doi.org/10.1073/pnas.0812525106

Preuss, T. M. (2012). Human brain evolution: From gene discovery to phenotype discovery. *Proceedings of the National Academy of Sciences, 109*(Supplement_1), 10709–10716. http://doi.org/10.1073/pnas.1201894109

Randerson, J. (2009). Fossil Ida : extraordinary find is 'missing link' in human evolution. *The Guardian*, pp. 1–4.

Rebourg, C., Chastanet, M., Gouesnard, B., Welcker, C., Dubreuil, P., & Charcosset, a. (2003). Maize introduction into Europe: the history reviewed in the light of molecular data. *TAG. Theoretical and Applied Genetics. Theoretische Und Angewandte Genetik, 106*(5), 895–903. http://doi.org/10.1007/s00122-002-1140-9

Rolian, C., Lieberman, D. E., & Zermeno, J. P. (2011). Hand biomechanics during simulated stone tool use. *Journal of Human Evolution, 61*(1), 26–41. http://doi.org/10.1016/j.jhevol.2011.01.008

Ruff, C. (2009). Relative limb strength and locomotion in homo habilis. *American Journal of Physical Anthropology, 138*(1), 90–100. http://doi.org/10.1002/ajpa.20907

Saracci, R. (2014). Concluding remarks. *Cancer Treatment and Research, 159*, 457–60. http://doi.org/10.1007/978-3-642-38007-5_26

Schoenemann, P. T. (2013). Hominid Brain Evolution. In *A Companion to Paleoanthropology* (pp. 136–164). Blackwell Publishing Ltd. http://doi.org/10.1002/9781118332344.ch8

Schrenk, F. (2013). Earliest Homo. In *A Companion to Paleoanthropology* (pp. 480–496). Blackwell Publishing Ltd.

Siegel, H. (2004). Faith, Knowledge and Indoctrination: A Friendly Response to Hand. *Theory and Research in Education, 2*(1), 75–83. http://doi.org/10.1177/1477878504040578

Silvertown, J. (2004). Plant coexistence and the niche. *Trends in Ecology and Evolution, 19*(11), 605–611. http://doi.org/10.1016/j.tree.2004.09.003

Sistiaga, A., Mallol, C., Galván, B., & Summons, R. E. (2014). The Neanderthal meal: A new perspective using faecal biomarkers. *Plos One, 9*(6), 6–11. http://doi.org/10.1371/journal.pone.0101045

Smith, M. P., & Harper, D. a T. (2013). Earth science. Causes of the Cambrian explosion. *Science, 341*(6152), 1355–6. http://doi.org/10.1126/science.1239450

Theunissen, B. (2012). Darwin and his pigeons. The Analogy between artificial and natural selection revisited. *Journal of the History of Biology, 45*(2), 179–212. http://doi.org/10.1007/s10739-011-9310-8

Toth, N. (1985). The oldowan reassessed: A close look at early stone artifacts. *Journal of Archaeological Science, 12*(2), 101–120. http://doi.org/10.1016/0305-4403(85)90056-1

Towe, K. M. (1970). Oxygen-collagen priority and the early metazoan fossil record. *Proceedings of the National Academy of Sciences of the United States of America, 65*(4), 781–788. http://doi.org/10.1073/pnas.65.4.781

Turner, A. H., Makovicky, P. J., & Norell, M. a. (2007). Feather quill knobs in the dinosaur Velociraptor. *Science (New York, N.Y.), 317*(5845), 1721. http://doi.org/10.1126/science.1145076

Urrutia-Fucugauchi, J., Camargo-Zanoguera, A., Pérez-Cruz, L., & Pérez-Cruz, G. (2011). The chicxulub multi-ring impact crater, yucatan carbonate platform, Gulf of Mexico. *Geofisica Internacional, 50*(1), 99–127.

Vandermeer, J. H. (1972). Niche Theory. *Annual Review of Ecology and Systematics, 3*(1), 107–132. http://doi.org/10.1146/annurev.es.03.110172.000543

Wadley, L. (2001). What is Cultural Modernity? A General View and a South African Perspective from Rose Cottage Cave. *Cambridge Archaeological Journal.* http://doi.org/10.1017/S0959774301000117

Weber, D. S., Stewart, B. S., & Lehman, N. (2004). Genetic Consequences of a Severe Population Bottleneck in the Guadalupe fur Seal (Arctocephalus townsendi). *Journal of Heredity, 95*(2), 144–153. http://doi.org/10.1093/jhered/esh018

Wenzel, G. W. (2009). Canadian Inuit subsistence and ecological instability - If the climate changes, must the Inuit? *Polar Research, 28*(1), 89–99. http://doi.org/10.1111/j.1751-8369.2009.00098.x

Whitman, W. B., Coleman, D. C., & Wiebe, W. J. (1998). Prokaryotes: the unseen majority. *Proceedings of the National Academy of Sciences of the United States of America, 95*(12), 6578–6583. http://doi.org/10.1073/pnas.95.12.6578

Wiens, J. J., Ackerly, D. D., Allen, A. P., Anacker, B. L., Buckley, L. B., Cornell, H. V., ... Stephens, P. R. (2010). Niche conservatism as an emerging principle in ecology and conservation biology. *Ecology Letters, 13*(10), 1310–1324. http://doi.org/10.1111/j.1461-0248.2010.01515.x

Wood, B., & Richmond, B. G. (2000). Human evolution: taxonomy and paleobiology. *Journal of Anatomy, 197* (Pt 1, 19–60. http://doi.org/10.1046/j.1469-7580.2000.19710019.x

Wrangham, R., & Conklin-Brittain, N. (2003). Cooking as a biological trait. *Comparative Biochemistry and Physiology - A Molecular and Integrative Physiology, 136*(1), 35–46. http://doi.org/10.1016/S1095-6433(03)00020-5

Wrangham, R. W., & Nishida, T. (1983). Aspilia spp . Leaves : A Puzzle in the Feeding Behavior of Wild Chimpanzees The University of Tokyo. *Primates, 24*(2), 276–282.

Index

Note: Page numbers followed by *t* indicate tables.

CPSIA information can be obtained
at www.ICGtesting.com
Printed in the USA
LVOW02s1455260717
542521LV00001BA/1/P

9 781524 940966